# HERE
# ON THIS
# HILL

D1571781

# HERE

# ON THIS

# HILL

*Conversations*
*with*
*Vermont Neighbors*

by
Linda S. Goldberg

Illustrations by
Helen Rabin

The Vermont Folklife Center
Middlebury, Vermont

The stone rubbing appearing in this book is adapted from
matching tombstones of Asa M. Bullock and Hannah Harwood
Bullock in the Dwinell Cemetery, Marshfield. The author's
home is on their land, one hundred years later.

Composition by Accura Type & Design.
Manufacturing by Northlight Studio Press.

Library of Congress Cataloging-in-Publication Data

Here on this hill : conversations with Vermont neighbors / by
    Linda S. Goldberg. — 1st ed.
        p.      cm.
    ISBN 0-916718-11-5 (trade pbk.) : $8.95
    1. Hollister Hill (Marshfield, Vt.)—Social life and customs.
2. Marshfield (Vt.)—Social life and customs.   3. Hollister Hill
(Marshfield, Vt.)—Biography.   4. Marshfield (Vt.)—Biography.
5. Interviews—Vermont—Marshfield.   6. Oral history.
I. Goldberg, Linda S. (Linda Shapiro), 1941-
F59.M43H47   1991                                91-11318
974.3'4—dc20                                         CIP

*To my sons,*
*Michael and Joshua,*
*who were raised on*
*Hollister Hill.*

Well, there I might live, I said; and
there I did live, for an hour, a summer
and a winter life; saw how I could let
the years run off, buffet the winter
through, and see the spring come in.

Henry David Thoreau, *Walden*

# TABLE OF CONTENTS

# ACKNOWLEDGMENTS

I WOULD LIKE TO THANK the following for their support of this work: my parents, Millie and Edward Shapiro, M.D.; David Goldberg; Ronald Blythe, whose book, *Akenfield* (Penguin, 1969), inspired mine; Priscilla Welsh; Mary Leahy; Leslie Parr and Jane C. Beck, the Vermont Folklife Center; Susan Bartlett Weber and Drusilla Macy, editors; Helen Rabin, illustrator; Mallory Lake, book designer; Noga Trevès Langfur and Alice Poremski, transcribers; Patty Edson, typist.

The following contributed to various stages of the work: Lucille Cerutti; Charlene Godin; Miff Keene; John Lamberton; R. Ruth Linden; Jaye Lindner; Charles T. Morrissey; Janet Nielsen; Mrs. Ruth Orton, former Town Clerk, Marshfield, Vermont; Eleanor Ott; Kären Pettersen; Helen and Tim Pitkin; Carol Rose; Michael Sherman, the Vermont Historical Society; Susan Zeigfinger; and, finally, Mrs. Clara Martin, who, unbeknownst to both of us, first awakened my curiosity about this area's history.

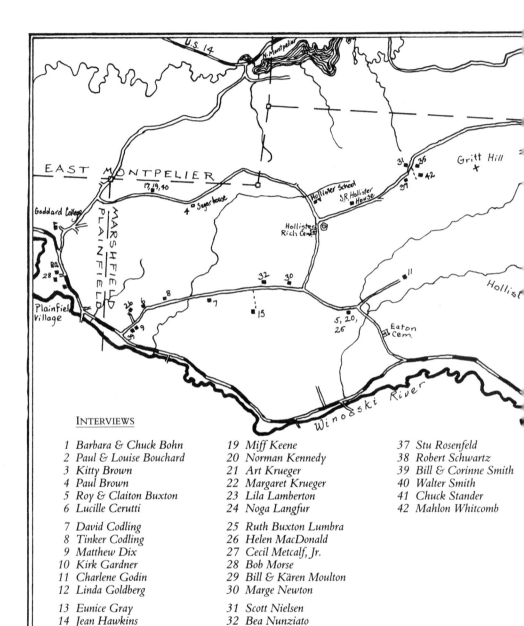

## INTERVIEWS

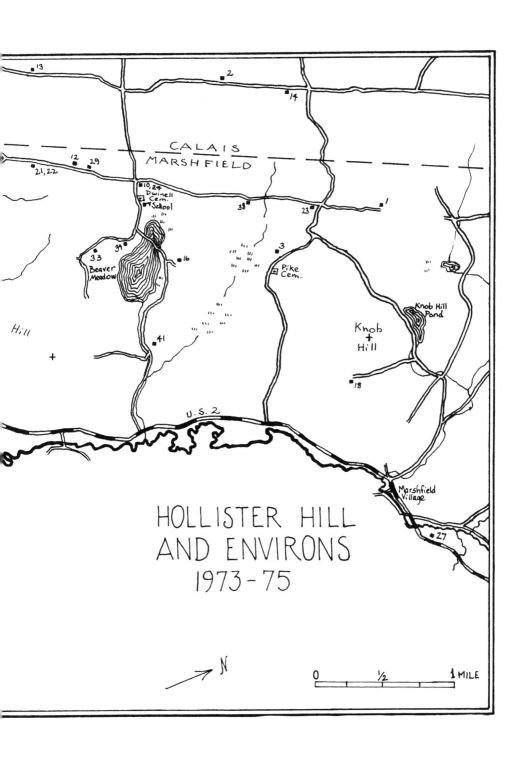

HOLLISTER HILL
AND ENVIRONS
1973-75

# Introduction

THERE WAS ONCE A TIME PRESENT, which is now past, and a place, where I still live, in which a dialogue occurred. Its participants included "old-timers," whose families had settled the most northwestern ridge of Marshfield between the end of the eighteenth and the beginning of the twentieth centuries, and "newcomers"—young, idealistic, college-educated, city-bred—who formed part of the "back-to-the-land" movement from the early 1960's to the mid 1970's. Goddard College, an experimental four-year college in neighboring Plainfield, offered a concentric attraction to newcomers from as early as the late 1930's.

Historically, this conflict between the old and new is neither original nor specific to this hilly region of central Vermont. For generations, territorial hunting and fishing boundaries were disputed by the Algonquin and Iroquois nations. The invasion of French and English settlers in the seventeenth and eighteenth centuries changed the extent of the antagonism, as well as the landscape, forever.

As the English gained geographic control, the Native Americans largely succumbed to European diseases or fled north and west, while the French were partially subsumed into the dominant culture. Through settlement and warfare the American Yankee eventually controlled the area that would become northern New England, creating a model for further continental exploration and establishment.

In the early nineteenth century, small towns were settled near natural resources—water power, lumber, granite—by "men of small fortunes and large families" (Zadock Thompson's *History of Vermont*, 1853) from New Hampshire, Massachusetts and Connecticut. Surrounding these self-contained villages were the hillside farms, created by hand-clearing seventy to eighty percent of Vermont's forests.

Economic and political change, which had been primarily local in the nineteenth century, was superseded by distant worldwide influences in the twentieth. But in the mid 1960's a measurable social dislocation occurred, an influx of "new" people with a "new" ideology—one based on the values of an older time, which local residents had variously retained or discarded. Predictably, conflict, as well as assimilation and conciliation, occurred between the descendents of the earlier settlers and those who formed the most recent immigration.

Curious about the effect of intruders such as myself on the established, rural population, I conducted interviews with my hillside neighbors from late 1973 to mid 1975. The resulting tapes and transcripts are housed in the Vermont Folklife Center, Middlebury, Vermont, and are accessible to interested students.

Although this work emphasizes contemporary perceptions and experiences, remnants of the past persist. The landscape remains visually rural although most of its occupants presently work away from the hill. The town's population of 1200 is approximately what it was one hundred years ago. "Neighboring" is still important. The individual is recognized for what he is—and isn't. Perhaps to be seen is the same as being loved.

Because life in northern New England is shaped by a harsh, often overwhelming climate, I have "fitted" (to use an older word) this perpetual human story of the invasion by the newcomer—and the old-timer's reaction—into a seasonal framework. Our human conflicts may be collective or individual, but the dominance of the natural world binds us all.

# *Late Fall*

THERE IS, FIRST, THE CHANGING OF THE LIGHT. The yellow light of the middle of the year is diminished as we turn our back to the sun. Below the quilted greyness of a November sky, the fields stand pale and still. Brown—that plainest of colors, the plainest sounding of colors—is everywhere multiplied in the trunks of trees, dead grasses, dropped leaves, the furred look of all dried vegetable matter.

The only constant in the weather is change. A sunstruck day in earliest November will turn to rain the next, with a light but steady snow the third. The back roads alternately freeze, become impassable with wet snow, ooze water like oil during a warm spell, then turn so slick with ice they mirror a pale sun.

The absence of leaves on trees lets blow the somber rain of November. By the middle of the month, rain solidifies into a snow. A dusting of snow, they call it, which makes protected patches of grass under a spruce tree, or under a parked car, seem very green, and the stones in the walls dividing the fields very dark.

Dirt roads become dusty after the first snowfall melts. Dry, colder days follow. As Canada geese veer south, chickadees pick dead insects from abandoned spider webs. A doe and her pair of young eat rotting cabbages in the garden.

November is the Janus of the northern year. Dogs furtively bury a bone; cats remember the stove. Humans scurry to cover woodpiles, put up storm windows, and bank old foundations with an inventive variety of wood, plastic, leaves, pine boughs or hay bales. The last carrot is dug, the last spring bulb planted.

Summer clothes vanish; long johns, wool socks and winter boots reappear. Hooks in the hall or ell are cluttered with heavy outerwear. Their breath visible when they run, children play a last game of kick-ball or touch football. They hurry to skate on the frozen ponds before the first staying snowstorm of winter.

The houses stand shut against the cold. The straight smoke of a stoked wood fire or the faint discharge of a furnace disturb the still air. The first icicles lengthen. Indoors, we prolong the sun's brief warmth by moving from the west side of the room to the east an hour before noon. The late-autumn light coming in the window, reflecting off inside walls, is white.

MRS. LILA LAMBERTON *lives alone in the large, weathered farmhouse at "the second four corners," which lead northward to Cabot, westward to East Calais, eastward to Marshfield Village, and southward down Hollister Hill. As the oldest interviewee, Mrs. Lamberton had the most direct connection with the formerly intact, but now largely invisible, world of the working hillside farm.*

## Lila Lamberton, 82

This place has been right in the Lamberton family, from one genera-tion to another, ever since 1853. These people originally came from over across with the early settlers. Roy's grandfather bought the place and built the main part of the house. I'm not a Lamberton, only by marriage, but I still keep the place. I have 120 acres here now.

I didn't always live on a farm when I was small. My people moved quite a lot here and there, wherever they thought they could do better. I didn't like to move, so I said, "If I'm ever fool enough to get married, I'll settle down and I'll stay right here." And I have lived up to that threat. I married the third day of January, 1911, and come here, and I've stayed here ever since — and probably will as long as I live.

We lived with Roy's folks for pretty near two years, but I don't approve of that kind of an arrangement. It's pretty hard for the younger generation to do things to suit the older ones. We never had any trouble, but we bought them out. From then on we carried on till he died here, in 1963, twenty-first of November.

The last few years we got along alone. We never hired much help. I helped him when I could. I didn't like housework; I preferred to work outdoors. I handled livestock and always kept a good garden. I haven't the last two years. I've got a little lettuce and some greens (I like greens awful well), and I grow string beans mixed in with the flowers.

When I was young, I wanted to study to be a doctor. My mother was so old-fashioned. She said, "Well, I never heard of women doctors." Of course, that made me want to go all the worse, but I didn't have the money to put me there, and they didn't have, so that's that. I just forgot about it. No, I haven't forgotten about it. It's followed me all my life. But I have settled down to doctorin' animals — I was always crazy for horses and cattle — and takin' care of my own family.

Only one thing: it's been a hard life. Roy used to have asthma. He was sick a lot, and that used him up. That meant more of my time outside and in the barn. Many times I've sat down and milked ten cows by hand. We never kept over fifteen. This isn't a very big farm.

When Roy talked of buyin' a milkin' machine, I said, "Buy it if you want it, but you run it, not me." And I never did. It seemed a lot of foolin' around for nothin'. Those milkin' machine pails were heavy. If you'd done it by hand, all you got to do is to go in there and sit down and take your pail between your knees and get hold of those tits and milk. Very simple thing to do. Yes! and it's better for the cows, too.

I learned to drive oxen when I was fourteen years old. My father didn't have a hired man in the sugar place, so I went out and helped scatter buckets. I took the ox team and gathered the sap. You could drive them just by talkin' to them. If you wanted to go right, you'd say, "Gee," and if you wanted to go left, it's "Haw." We had a number of different pairs after I came here. Pete and Mike, the last pair we had, were handy and trusty. They'd stand and wait for you all day.

Everybody used to have a pig. They thought they couldn't get along without they had their salt pork in the wintertime. In a tight pinch I'd help to butcher off, but he had to shoot the pig. I don't believe in stickin' a pig and lettin' them die by inches. We used to put our hams down in what we called a pickle. I've still got the recipe. There's nothin' better than a nice slice of salt pork. You roll it in flour and fry it until it's crisp and brown. Not too brown, but until it's done, I might say. You don't know what's good if you've never tasted of it. I wish I had some now.

I don't know as I can tell you much more. It's too bad that you couldn't have been along here a few years before this to get the real facts of Hollister Hill. When Roy and I come here, there was just one place that wasn't being carried on as some sort of a farm. Every family was well-fixed and comfortable and had income enough to get them along. It makes me sick the way the farms have gone. I've enjoyed visitin' with you, but I haven't learned much about your history. How did you ever come to this country?

RUTH BUXTON LUMBRA *was born in 1903. Her family's farm was located "just down over the hill, the other side of the woods, from the George Hollister property"—thereby forming a direct connection with the area's wealthiest family, after whose large land holdings the hill was called. Mrs. Lumbra left the farm to continue her education, teach school, and*

*marry. While she was teaching in a one-room school in Montgomery, Vermont, the most documented event in Vermont's recent history—the flood of November 6 and 7, 1927—occurred.*

## Ruth Buxton Lumbra, 72

The early settlers took the high land. At that time there was less sickness if you were away from the river. You were safe from the Indians when they'd come up the Winooski River. Alonzo Buxton first owned the old farm on Hollister Hill. Oh, 'twas in our family a hundred years anyway. The Jake Martin place was just beyond our land, and the Eben Dodge place was the third one. That Eben Dodge place was the original property when the Town of Marshfield was settled. It was passed down through one family seven or eight generations. You just think: the Indians owned that land and it never was put up for sale until 1970. There were not very many boys; it came down through the womenfolks.

Hollister Hill got its name from that beautiful brick house up there hardly out of sight of the Hollister Hill School. It was a very sightly place. The Hollisters were highly respected people, they and the land. They owned much more land than Hollister Hill. They owned back pastures over by Hardwood and Jerusalem and the Devil's Hopyard and the Cream Pot. When my father, John Brooks Buxton, was a young man, he went up crosslots to Hollister's and worked year after year drivin' a yoke of oxen.

It used to be likin' it to a holiday when the springtime word would be sent around among the neighbors that George Hollister was movin' his young cattle on to the mountain pasture. Everybody knew that if Hollister's drove was goin' through, there'd be better than forty, fifty cattle. Perhaps the followin' day, two or three of the neighbors would drive a lesser number of cattle to summer pasture.

My three brothers and I traveled those mountainsides all our lifetimes with young cattle. They had to be salted and counted every week. I handled the horse to take salt over and look up your calves and your cattle and count them and come home and go back again on another Sunday. Those days were a picnic to us. They made a change from the other six days of the week.

Girls were supposed to just help the mothers, but my interest was outdoors. I was the oldest one, the "best boy." That was why I helped with the heavy team and was given the horse to get to the villages. I used to take the cream from my father's herd of cattle every other day to North Montpelier where butter was made. I either rode or drove the horses to the blacksmith shop for their shoeing.

I started school in Plainfield Village when I was six years old. There was only five to graduate from the eighth grade when I did. When we went into high school we went Plainfield way, then the last two years over to Goddard Seminary in Barre, which is now Goddard College. The principal, O.K. Hollister, advised me to take teacher training because of the shortage of teachers. You could get a position quicker than a stenographer or bookkeeper.

I did five years in rural schools. I taught at the Horn of the Moon School in East Montpelier and the Hazen Notch School in Montgomery. It was so rugged up there, school started the 20th of July and was closed through January and February. When I got married, my husband was one of the workers in the tub shop there in Montgomery. His father was the boss tubmaker. They made maple veneer and butter tubs, from five-pound tubs to fifty-pound tubs. A day's work would be three, four hundred tubs. It was a flourishing business.

I was up there in Montgomery until after the 1927 flood. My father and mother suffered, not because anything was wrong at the farm—Hollister Hill is high land—but because my brothers were out in Mechanicville, New York. My brothers had been home two weeks before and had got my father's Dodge automobile. My youngest brother came home to enter the University of Vermont, which left two brothers out there at the date of the flood.

This is the story that my people have always enjoyed tellin' 'bout the

Dodge. The day before the flood affected Vermont the worst, my brothers left the Albany area and crossed the Hudson River. They noticed that the water was high and that it was swift and more rugged than when they'd been across other times during the summer. But they thought that they would head for home. As they got nearer the Vermont border, they were advised to turn back. But my middle brother, Roy, was a good driver and a good mechanic, and he was determined to get to Vermont.

They crossed below Rutland into Vermont. The road was impassable and cars were stopped, and they were asked not to go on sometimes, but the old Dodge kept a-goin' and they got to Burlington. They immediately went to my youngest brother's address to stay overnight. Then they joined a caravan that was goin' over Smugglers' Notch and got into Waterbury.

My oldest brother had worked in Waterbury at the hardware store, so he went to his former employer and asked if he could—park the Dodge!—in the backyard. In the automobile were their summer belongings and two wedding presents, large pictures of *The Blue Boy*. One was for a cousin, and the other was for Joe Bartlett of Plainfield.

The brothers started afoot from Waterbury to North Montpelier. They came through in one day. There weren't any roads, but they knew the lay of the land. They crawled on their hands and knees across fields and pastures. They came around North Montpelier, then up over by the Hollister Hill School.

My father and mother hadn't heard from any of the boys. My mother put a light in the kitchen window for a beacon. She felt 'twas the right thing to do. About the third night that she had the light lighted, she saw the boys comin'. One of them crawled to the doorstep and straightened out on the floor. The other one sat down on the old stone. They couldn't have gone much further.

I want to make sure I tell about finding the old Dodge late in the fall. 'Twas left at least a month, perhaps longer. There wasn't one thing ever touched or disturbed in that automobile. When they got the doors open, those two pictures were in perfect condition. I was reminded of my brothers' gift to this Joe Bartlett when I was at his funeral last Monday, because it crossed a lot of water between New York and Vermont.

HERE AGAIN IS THE FLOOD, *followed by the 1929 Depression, the 1938 hurricane, World War II, and the early 1950's — a decade before the arrival of the "back-to-the-land" generation. This portrait of Stubby Robertson is based on two interviews, about a year apart. Within that time, Stubby had diminished from an active man to a coughing, exhausted semi-invalid. Like many granite workers, he had contracted silicosis.*

## Stubby Robertson, 61

My father and my uncle came to Hardwick from Maine in 1906 or '7. My father was a granite man. He put forty years in the granite shed, all told. Granite was most of the people's livelihood around this particular part of the country.

He married my mother, and I was born in 1912 in Hardwick. I was brought up in a little settlement a mile from the village. We called it

Mackville. There was a rural school right there. I was an average student—nothing elaborate, just getting by. I liked school. I wouldn't miss a day of school any more than I would miss a day of work when I first started working.

When I was in the sixth grade, my father thought he wanted to be a farmer. So he rented a farm up outside of Hardwick and had ten, eleven cows. Got up early in the morning and milked the cows, come home at night and milked the cows, go back and forth to the shed. He was going to buy the farm from the old lady that owned it.

My father had almost paid for it lock, stock and barrel in rent. That was about the time these French people were coming down from Canada with all kinds of money and buying up property in Vermont. This French guy come along and offered this lady a lot more. The old lady couldn't refuse it, of course, so my family had to move back to Mackville.

In the fall of '27 the flood came. It rained so long the dams broke in Mackville Pond and Nichols Pond and East Long Pond. There was no warning. Water started undermining our house. I run the Model-T Ford up to the hill. It was all over by ten o'clock. All we saved was what clothes we had on our back and a wheelbarrow. Later we didn't find hardly as much as a spoon that we could identify.

All this water and mud went through the granite sheds and stopped all production. Men like my father had to work as a common laborer, which was smaller pay, for quite a period of time. There was no welfare and no unemployment benefits. There was a certain class of people, which there always was and always will be, that do need assistance. Everybody knew if you got any aid. It was in the Town Report. My folks never was on the town. We had cows and chickens and raised our own beef and pork. We cut our own wood. About all we ever needed was a little bit of money to buy some grain.

I didn't go back to school after the flood, by the way, because what clothes I had was what people give me, and they weren't quite suitable for high school. I quit school and worked out on farms and in the woods until I was sixteen. The day after I was sixteen I went to work in the granite sheds. They were back operating that next spring.

My folks got on their feet fairly well in '29. The granite business was good. I was working, my father was working. My mother boarded people. We traded the Model-T for a 1926 Star; then we traded the Star for a brand-new '29 Nash automobile, in '29, 'bout as good a one as there was in the neighborhood. That was when people started using their credit.

It was rough all through Depression, but I worked. My father worked fairly good. In '32 the Democrats come around before the election to all the poor people and gave them blankets and commodities to get their votes. That was the way the Democrats got Roosevelt in.

My father worked one shift when this WPA started. They allowed him $9 every two weeks. From that $9 we'd get a bag of grain, some flour and sugar. The government give people the opportunity to work to keep from giving them the money outright, that's all. Times were really rough. In 1934 I worked to a gas station in Hardwick, seven days and seven evenings, for $12 a week. I paid my mother $5 a week board, and I run a car, and I saved $65 during the summer.

After I got out of the gas station, I went back to the stone sheds, off and on, when they worked. In them days they didn't work steady like they do today. The spring of the year was a rush season for monuments before Decoration. That was really a boom time. After Decoration there was quite a lull in business.

Along about '36 it was bad times. I leased a gas station in Hardwick and went into business for myself. The '38 hurricane affected Hardwick, all right. The government paid people to draw hurricane pulp right in back of my gas station. This fellow come along one day and said, "They're gonna ship this pulp away in cars. Why don't you do the job?" I said, "I don't know anything about pulp." "Well," he said, "they're gonna have some bids on it."

I needed the money, so I asked some of my customers what I should do, and I sent my bid in. I'll be darned if I didn't get the contract to load all the pulp. I was pretty comical. The government man said, "I suppose you've done this a long time," and I said, "Oh, yeah, no problem at all." I shipped out 137 carloads of pulp. I made about $1,200 in twelve weeks, which was a lot of money in them days.

I continued that gas station until '42. When the war broke out, they started rationing and everybody was gone in the service. I wasn't taken because I was over twenty-eight. People would come in and say, "Well, I just heard from my son. How come you're not in the service?" After months of that, you get where you kind of hate to see those people come in.

My bank account was getting awful low and I said, "I really want to go." So I went. I don't say I was in love with the service, but I was fortunate to be stationed in Hartford, Connecticut, with the Eastern Defense Command. At the time of the Battle of the Bulge, I was sent overseas. New Year's Day of '45, I was on the boat. I was in France a year and three months.

My first wife, Eva, and I built a new garage in Hardwick after the war. Then I remarried, and my second wife, Bea, and I come over here

to Marshfield in '53. I eventually went back into the shed. I put twelve, fourteen more years in granite, grinding tools and finally learning the polishing trade. Coarse granite winds up to be a polished mirror surface you can see your face in. It's quite an accomplishment.

It's definitely hard work. It's not the highest-paying job in the country—only a minimum wage. You've got to work thirty years in the granite sheds and be 65 years old or disabled, then you can't draw on but $80 a month pension. I have a small shed pension now. This place is going to be my boy's heritage. It's not much, but it's all we got.

"GOT YOUR DEER YET?" *is the refrain heard on the back roads as one car of plaid-jacketed hunters slowly passes another during the last two weeks of November. Although some women hunt, most acknowledge their yearly abandonment by cleaning out closets or completing a forgotten sewing project. The hunters hope to return with a stiff deer tied like a trophy to the hood of the car. Later, the carcass is strung up outside where men, talking quietly and smoking, stand looking at it.*

*Hunting is what Bill Moulton, a forester with the Vermont Department of Forests and Parks, looks forward to all year. Although his wife, Kären, who's a landscape architect with the same department, used to hunt, she usually spends Thanksgiving with her family on Long Island, New York.*

## Bill and Kären Moulton, 28 and 26

BILL: I started hunting with my father when I was about twelve. He stuck me out and said, "Stay here until you see something." I got nervous and fidgety two hours later. He didn't pay much attention to me the rest of the season. I was more or less on my own. You wander around and learn a little bit each year. I'd estimate to become a hunter takes ten or twelve years.

KÄREN: When I became sixteen, my father bought me a rifle for Christmas. It didn't make any difference if I was a girl or a boy. I was the oldest; that's why I was chosen. I automatically went hunting without thinking because my father said to go. And I enjoyed it. That first year I was going to be tough just like all the men. I really didn't know what was going on. I was scared when I had to walk by myself, but my father was always over the hill, watching.

We'd hunt with drivers and standers. Somebody places the standers out into the woods, usually on a straight line. An equal number of drivers walk through the woods, trying to maintain some distance between themselves, until they meet up with the standers. The purpose is to push the deer towards the standers who are supposed to shoot at them.

BILL: There's somewhat of an art to being in the place you suspect a deer might come through, but there's no way of predicting where they will go. Every time you go out it's a different experience. You punish yourself to the point of exhaustion and come back frozen and cold and wet and hungry, but you've got just one thing on your mind. Its single purpose makes it a totally relaxing thing. It's the only time I can really unwind.

Half the fun is spending a week at a deer camp with friends. Everybody's really psyched up the first weekend of the season. By the time that last weekend comes, you're drained. All you think is: I don't want to shoot one of those damn things because then I'll have to clean it and take it home and butcher it. It takes a full day to butcher a deer properly.

Hunting's not a necessity like it was fifteen years ago in this state. When I was young, most of the people I knew depended on hunting for part of their winter food supply. To butcher a cow was a last resort. Nobody thought of buying beef. The supermarket chains have been the importers of beef.

You've got to know a little about the history of deer in Vermont. At the time the settlers came, there were square miles of nothing but dense forest canopy. There were very few deer because deer thrive on open areas. The Indians burned out quite a bit of land to encourage wildlife. I guess they were the first wildlife managers.

Back around 1900 there may have been five deer in the entire state. In the early 1900's they imported twelve pairs from Michigan. It took quite a few years to build up the population to a sizeable amount. I remember hearing some of the old-timers tell about driving forty miles to see a deer in someone's back pasture.

The deer herd mushroomed in the '40's and peaked back around 1966. At that time there were far more deer in the state than the land could handle. They ate off all the available food in their wintering areas. As a consequence, the food supply has never replenished itself. This has caused a general decline in the size and health of the herd. They estimate 10,000 get shot, 40,000 die of starvation every spring.

The argument the Fish and Game Department has is, Why have 40,000 dead deer every spring when they could be used for food? You could kill all the buck in the state and you'd still get mass starvation. There are a tremendous number of does per buck right now. The only way they could harvest them would be a doe season.

But the farmers traditionally remember the peak years in the '60's: "I can remember back when I was a kid we used to see forty deer out in that field. Today we don't see five." The uproar is because of the doe season. But the animal population peaked and destroyed the food cycle, which has never been allowed to build up again. Humans are the only control that's effective.

KÄREN: But some people don't want to shoot doe.

BILL: There's a real change in the attitude of the hunter when there's a doe season. People are a lot less discriminating about how they shoot and what they shoot at. No longer do you have to look for horns. This is what scares farmers and local people.

The rutting season changes deer habits completely. The bucks will continually fight and roam from one pack of does to another. They've got one thing on their minds and lose their caution. Supposedly, the rutting season hadn't started yet in Vermont this year. It's a handy excuse if you don't get a deer. I didn't ask any deer if they were rutting. I've had an exceptionally lucky year. Most people are lucky if they see a deer. I almost got a fourth one. The people I was with were ready to take my bullets away.

A deer hunter is a professional at telling how he killed one deer in ten different ways. Everybody's got countless stories about strange things that happened. I've heard of people shooting an antler and stunning a deer, and, thinking he's dead, putting him in the trunk, and then hearing this thing banging around in the back end trying to get out. Then you go to a gas station and ask the guy to check the air in your spare.

Everybody gets to talking about the one they killed close to the car so they didn't have to drag it. The one I heard that really topped them all was this: A guy could see a deer peering over a ledge. He leaned out the window and blasted him, and the deer came rolling over the ledge and landed right in the back of his pickup truck.

I heard a good one! This guy that works in my office had a brother who broke his arm two weeks before the season started. Opening day he walked across a brush pile. Unbeknownst, a bear was sleeping in the brush pile and stood up. The bear trampled him trying to get out of there and broke the same arm again. The guy couldn't get a shot at the bear, but he had a story to tell.

KÄREN: That's one of the reasons I gave up hunting. I just could not stand those stories.

KITCHEN STORIES, *revealed while a housewife cooks a meal, are as telling as those about hunting. The Godins — Charlene, Jean and three daughters — live across the road from the Buxton home place, in a farmhouse provided because Jean is the herdsman on what was the former Hollister farm. Charlene talked about cooking and her history while preparing Thanksgiving dinner for thirty-eight family members.*

## Charlene Godin, 28

My mom always had big Thanksgiving dinners. Holidays are very depressing if there's not a lot of people around. From so many in the family, I feel lonesome if I'm not with somebody. Grammy had sixteen children. Her house was spotless; the kids were never allowed in the house. That made my mom feel insecure and unloved. She first got married when she was fifteen, and was pregnant then. She was just too young. She wanted to do everything when she was tied down with all us kids—five of us and two from her second marriage.

My mom and I didn't get along too well. From the time I was nine I started babysitting out. I quit school when I was eleven and took care of kids and cleaned houses. When I was fourteen I went to Connecticut, then to Boston. When I come home from Boston, I started high school in Hardwick. I was in the ninth grade. I went to live with my stepfather and took care of my two stepbrothers. There was a story started that I was sleeping with my stepfather. It made me awful mad. It wasn't true at all.

That left awful feelings in the family, so I got a job working as a waitress. I couldn't serve drinks; I wasn't old enough. I met my first husband and got married to him when I was sixteen. Now that I'm older, I see that it was wanting a home and someone to take care of me. He was ten years older than me. I got pregnant three months after I got married. I didn't know anything about birth control then. We only was married two years. He drank. I didn't care for it at all, so I left him. I was then eighteen.

I went to work for my uncle in his restaurant in Hardwick. That's where I met Jean. Jean used to get a drink there. He was very quiet and mysterious-looking. That makes a woman more intrigued to know him. And I got to know him. I was pregnant for Kimberly, so we decided to get married. Don't talk very much, Jean. I'm the one that does all the talking.

I'm taking the fat off the ham because I've got it scored. I bought this ham. Jean raised five pigs, but we just sent them to be corn-smoked. We raise our own pigs, our own beef, and chickens. Jean chops off their heads — I don't think I could kill anything — and we both pluck the feathers off. I do the insides because Jean gets nauseated. Men are weak.

I take it for granted that everybody knows how to do some canning. They don't. My mom always did seven, eight hundred quarts every fall: string beans and carrots and spinach and swiss chard and beets, pickled and regular, and all kinds of pickles. The things I raise in my garden, my mom didn't. She's not much on finding out about different things. And me, I like to try everything. I don't think I'm going to have enough time and energy in my life to do all the things that I want to.

My problem is that what I do isn't that special — that anyone, any dummy, can do it. I was the black sheep in my family. I've always felt inferior. Yet everybody says I have a nice personality. I agree with them there, because I try to get along with everybody. I wouldn't want anyone to dislike me.

Now, let's see, we've got to make the rolls. I want to make some sweet rolls and plain rolls. When I make rolls, I don't go by the recipe. I can tell by the texture if it's going to be all right. My mom says I cook like my Grandmother Quinn. She didn't care for my Grandmother Quinn. She says, "Oh, you slop everything together," she says, "you don't measure a thing." And I say, "Yeah, but everything comes out fairly well."

Directions bother me. I'm not going to be told what to do. Yet my husband tells me what to do all the time. If he comes in the house, he wants me here. He doesn't want me to work out, see. I have been thinking I might go to work. Not for the money — the money isn't nothing — but just to be with people.

I'm scraping off the shelf here so that I can do my pie crusts. I'm going to make six pies: one will be mincemeat and two will be cherry and two will be pumpkin and one will be raisin cream. But I'm wondering if I should bother, you know? I like everything to be just right, but I'm fighting with myself to decide if it's worth the bother.

Look at me: here I am twenty-eight and feel like I've had all the weight of the world on my shoulders. I should have had time to grow up more so that I could have been a kid—just be a kid. I missed something and I want for it, maybe.

HAVING LIVED FOR YEARS *on Walter Smith's farm, Miff Keene helps with chores, mends fence, and daily cleans the hens' eggs with an old rag. He says, "I feel sad in the fall, when the leaves fall down and the geese go south, because every leaf represents a person dyin'."*

## Miff Keene, 53

I was born in Russell, New York. My folks bought a farm in Woodbury, Vermont, when I was three years old. I started workin' 'bout quick as I got big enough to walk: carryin' a milk pail, weedin' the garden. Later, I helped my father on the farm. Pickin' the stones I wasn't too happy with, especially when they were boulders that would take three men to roll on to a stone boat. The farm was very, very stony. Most of them were.

I started school when I was five. This was early, but my folks thought I might as well get started. I can't say as I enjoyed school. I never could stand English. This foolishness about verbs and proverbs and nouns was very hard for me. Arithmetic was hard, and spelling I was fair on, but history was my choice. Geography was hard enough, time you learnt all your countries and their capitals, but I enjoyed that.

I never regretted not goin' to high school. I got out in the eighth grade, and I've learned a hang of a lot more since. When the school bus came to take my sister to high school, I was never so happy in my life. I was free! I was sprung! I said, "You poor suckers, you're stuck in that damn schoolhouse." You know what I did? I took a pail and went into the woods and picked blackberries.

I love to be in the woods. I've always been a hunter, ever since I was fourteen. We had to shoot deer for our meat because we couldn't afford to kill a cow. I can feel a deer lookin' at me if I haven't seen it yet. The sixth sense, you might call it.

I have had experiences that I would hesitate to tell many people. There's an old pasture over to Woodbury. I'd fixed fence and I'd hunted right in that pasture for years. One day in the afternoon, right about now, I was huntin' deer and went by this old cellar hole. I froze right in my tracks; I couldn't take another step. I couldn't help but feel that the spirits of the people that had lived there resented anybody bein' there. Can you understand that?

And I'll tell you somethin' which may sound foolish to you, but when I go into this old pasture once a year to visit, I stop at the gate and ask permission to walk in. I get down on my knees and pray. This sounds crazy, doesn't it? But if I do that, the spirits won't bother me. Which is probably ridiculous to anybody else, but it's my way.

I had a rare happenstance: I was walkin' along through a field, a field I used to own, and felt a power pullin' my legs right down into the ground. I could hardly move one leg ahead of the other. After I got pretty near to the car, it let go of me. How do you figure that one out? I feel the land wanted me to stay. How could I? I had to come back and go to work.

Have you ever experienced feelin' the presence of a dead person in the room with you? After my father died, I'd finished chores, and my mother and I were settin' in our livin' room. All of a sudden she looked at me, and I looked at her. Dad's presence was there: he was standin' right behind my chair. I said, "Don't be afraid, it's just Dad." And she said, "I know it."

My mother experienced the same thing in New York State before I was born. Her mother was dyin'. My father was to the barn to do his barn work. My mother was up with her mother when she heard the kitchen door open and shut. She wondered how come Dad had got done so quick and come in. She came down, but he wasn't there. When he came in, she asked if he'd come in for somethin', and he said no. Well, you know what that was, don't you? 'Twas Death enterin' the house. Death opened and shut the door and came for my grand-mother. She died that night.

You can welcome death. I died once. When I was twenty-seven, I had a heart attack. When you're dyin', you can hear water runnin' like a heavy river. I could hear it. I couldn't speak. I couldn't move. Luck-ily, a nurse gave me a shot in the arm which brought me back to this side. But I know what 'tis to die. If you're not killed instantly, you'll hear the big river runnin'.

# *Winter*

DEER SEASON IS OVER THE SUNDAY AFTER THANKSGIVING. Winter begins on Monday. A pale sun, pale as a moon, won't be seen before seven. The sky is grey, the light dark, the day silent. It is dusk when the afternoon school bus unloads snow-suited children. There is a sure darkness by four o'clock. From the hill the Christmas lights in the village are already visible.

There is no one kind of snow, nor snowfall. A steady snow is sometimes hard and granular, sometimes soft and powdery (the easiest to shovel, the best for skiing), sometimes heavy and wet. A warm and windy snow will be thrown against one side of the trees where its whiteness spreads, fungus-like. To walk in this softness is to sink up to your hip joints. Occasionally, the wind will scoop fine snow so that it falls, amazingly, up.

The big storms start innocently enough. The morning temperature's in the 20's; the grey clouds have congealed into a grey sky. You look, but see nothing. You look again— intermittent whiteness. Soon, the hypnotic snow overwhelms the landscape. The edges of the road disappear into the woods, driveways lose their openings into the road, cars are abandoned in driveways. Large, slow flakes signal the end of the storm.

The morning after there is a spectacular dawn, then pure blue light to show the living day. Every tree is covered with a bending-down whiteness until the lowest pine branches disappear. The snow has plumped up the fields and buries the sound of the snowplow on the road. In the woods a dog leaves tracks the shape of flying birds. After a few warmer days, tree branches will suddenly spring to release their weight of snow. But the wind will rise, the day will harden until the fields have a satiny sheen and trees crack in the cold.

A few days before the typical "January thaw," people come down with colds and flu. The thaw melts the lower end of small ponds and marshes, which suddenly show some dark, running water between snowy banks. A few tufts of miraculous green weeds surface. The hills are the shade of a newborn's eyes — very dark, not clearly one color.

Still, no one would be foolish enough not to prepare for the duration. Kids, nagged, fill the woodbox. On freezing nights you listen as you sleep. A light backdraft from a changing wind will bang open the damper, waking you. You check the fire. The almost-burned log is grey and furry like some hibernating animal. You feed the stove, then run the water so the pipes won't freeze, before returning to your cooled bed. It is later that you half-consciously reach down to pull off your socks.

To rise before a late dawn tries the hardiest; returning up the hill in second gear is an act of desperation. There is nothing as reassuring as the sight of cows through the small, fogged windows of a neighbor's barn, or of the rectangular light falling from your own windows onto the snow. Not even the dog hears your silent return until you stamp on the porch. Coming into a warm house shocks the system. Your cheeks redden; your pale thighs turn pink and itchy; your muscles relax. Unless it is necessary to leave, you will stay home.

Routine-deadened days and solitary nights cause that most common mid-winter affliction: cabin fever. Even cheerful people — those who can hardly wait for the ponds to freeze or for the first skiing snowfall — suffer. Pessimists tend to hate "the ugly white stuff." Introspective souls welcome the silence, yet feel constricted by the beginning of February. All are grateful for basics: running water, a car that starts, a sunny day, any form of communication, hot cider and popcorn, jigsaw puzzles, seed catalogs, a good apple, hope.

Visibly longer days release the earth's hidden aliveness by the third week in February. Small flocks of starlings prematurely huddle on the road. Poplar trunks are quite green against the purplish-grey of the maples. The tips of white birches tend towards red. In the mid-day light, weeping willows stand golden. No longer draped by heavy snow, broken corn stalks stand up from the fields. On a mild week-end, houses will suddenly pour out skiers, shoppers, walkers, woodpile-sorters, snowmobilers. The longest season, winter, comes undone slowly, like a boot lace untying as you walk.

As a largely uninhabited landscape *in the early eighteenth century attracted Vermont's first white settlers, those who arrived during the twentieth came for much the same reason — to act out one's destiny outside conventional restraints. But fourteen hours of darkness daily, over three months, grants us time to recall our origins, test our endurance, and question remaining in a landscape abandoned by glaciers, yet shaped by the cold.*

*Within the community, Helen Pitkin is inextricably linked with her husband, Tim Pitkin, and with Goddard College, which he established in Plainfield. Still, Helen was once a newcomer. Her family left the South, where Helen was born, to return to Vermont during the second decade of this century. Helen's precise memory allows us to view an individual's history within the family context.*

## Helen Pitkin, 72

This is my family history. It's tied in with genealogy. Three branches of my family got to the North American continent before 1805. They came from Scotland and from England. It's the same old story of overpopulation: somebody had to go. They were adventuresome. My father's family didn't look for a comfortable place; they looked for an opportunity. All of their children eventually settled up in the Northeast Kingdom.

That sense of adventure has helped me to dare to do what ought to be done. I think it's this seeing a situation, evaluating it and thinking, "This is the next step." So many persons, probably rightfully so, won't give up this job and take another because of Social Security. My father would have thumbed his nose at Social Security.

He started lumbering up in the Northeast Kingdom here. Then, in 1895 or '6, maybe earlier, he moved to West Virginia, in Tucker County, where I was born. My family was literally helping hew this community out of the wilderness. The tree stumps were as high as the houses behind them.

But both my father and mother had grown up in Vermont, and they thought it would be ideal to go back where the grass was green and people were people. I was fourteen when we came to Vermont, in 1915, during the "back-to-the-land" movement.

The farm we were on was not what you'd call a good farm, and my father was no farmer. All we did was cut the hay and raise potatoes and carrots. I changed my mind about what I was going to do in college because I thought our farm was located in an ideal place to have a small fruit farm. It would make a better income for all of us.

I transferred from the College of Liberal Arts at the University of Vermont to the College of Agricultural Science. I was the one girl in a class of twenty-two boys. I knew the boys as persons who could do what I could do. It's this background that led me to expect marriage to be a very comfortable being together with the person you wanted most to be with.

In the summer, the crowd of us would arrange what we called a Victrola dance, where we'd take our own records and the Victrola. In the winter, Mother would invite the snowshoe club up to our house. Now, our house was a little house, but there would be thirty, thirty-

five people. We'd bring our own sandwiches, but Mother served baked beans and cocoa (we raised our own beans and we had our own milk). And she always had special table decorations. I remember one time she made a girl on snowshoes and a boy on skis on this absorbent-cotton hill in the center of the table.

Mother was sort of an ageless person. She was very happy with older people, but she loved to have young people around. My mother was a happy individual. As I look back, she had no business to be happy many, many days. She had things to cope with that other women, I know, would not have coped with as my mother did. I always admired my mother because she enabled us to grow up so comfortably. I suppose without realizing it, I adopted her philosophy and adapted it to my own situation.

We first came to the hill about forty years ago when Tim was in public-school work. We spent the summers in the house built by my husband's grandfather before 1845. There was no electricity. There was no pump. Water came from a spring, through the dips and over the ledges, and would often get air locks. Water trickled twenty-four hours a day into a water barrel. To conserve water, we would save the rinse water from the dishes to soak the children's play clothes in.

The lights were all kerosene, which had to be filled, and the chimneys washed, every day. We cooked on a three-burner oil stove. There was a portable oven that would cover two burners. One ten-day period there were eleven of us, and I baked twenty-two loaves of bread with that stove. It was during that same time that I made five gallons of root beer from extract. You put the bottles on their side on the floor of a cool place and turned them the first three days. Then it could be put down-cellar. It wasn't poured over ice because we had no ice.

I began baking bread forty years ago, and I have baked practically all our bread ever since. We liked it well enough so I often baked in the afternoon to have warm bread and jelly for dessert. We always did and still do have a garden. You had fresher vegetables, and it was an economical thing to do. One day Tim called the children, and they all went out and picked beans. Then we all pulled the stems and helped cut up. We canned thirty-five quarts of string beans that day. That was a real day's work, I thought.

Life was busier when the children were small. All my darning and hand sewing I did at night, so I was available for conversation if Tim wanted to talk. I was able to sit down in the evening and rest enough so that I didn't feel pressure that I know many young women say they feel. I am not patting myself on the back for this; it just was my good fortune not to feel encumbered.

Tim was a supervising principal and had to go to South Wallingford to visit a school. Down there was a woman who was the wife of a dairy tester. He was gone six days a week. They didn't have a phone. She didn't have the conveniences: no electricity, no water pump. Anyway, I knew she was lonesome, so I would ride with my children to see her. She had seven children, none of them in high school yet. One day I went to the door and she said, "Am I glad to see you. I am so sick of talking with nobody but Edith Walters, I'm ready to throw the children out of the house." Her name was Edith Walters. This gave me a different perspective about how busy I was.

A woman has a responsibility for developing her own inner resources that she didn't have time to do when she was washing by hand and ironing with a flat iron. This is not an easy thing to do. Many of the young people have been so exposed to television and advertising and novels, if they've read anything, that they think that when they've exchanged marriage vows everything is going to be rosy. When her husband comes home, it's her extra business to keep him involved with the family and with her and with the community.

The other day a service-station man was pumping gas and said, "How are you?" And I said, "Well, I don't tell all to everybody, but," I said, "really, I have had a pretty good life." And he said, "Well, I'm glad to hear that. That's not true of everybody that stops here."

ONE HUNDRED AND FIFTY YEARS *after Helen Pitkin's ancestors left Scotland for this country, Norman Kennedy arrived in the United States from his native Aberdeen. Invited to tour the East as a folksinger and storyteller in 1965, Norman eventually established a weaving school in what had been the Buxtons' home place.*

## Norman Kennedy, 41

My mother's clan and my father's clan — the Bruces and the Kennedys — were renowned fighters in the old days. They were used to decidin' what they wanted and fightin' for it. They're not sheepy people. I'm the oldest son of the oldest son. I was born in my grandparents' house. I was the oldest grandchild, so the older people took me over when my mother started to work. When you've got kids brought up by their parents, they'll never learn a bloody thing. You need to learn the culture of your own people from your grandparents.

My father used to take my brother and myself out on a Sunday. He'd walk our feet off around the town. We were raised within walking distance of where all the grandparents and great-grandparents were born. My folk have lived in the same area since the early 1300's. There are bound to be stories come up. We had our eyes open to listen to some of the talk. Half the time they were talkin' about things that happened a couple of hundred years ago. That stuff soaks in if you're interested.

We were not churchy people. Jesus Christ! We see the trouble religion makes. We all steered clear of that stuff except for an uncle who got a chance to be a minister. It was either that or the shipyards. He was wise enough to know that if he took the ministry, he'd have a damn-sight easier life. It was pure economics.

My father used to say, "It's hard times that makes character." He left school at fourteen. There was no point in goin' on. If you were lucky, you got a trade. His father was in the shipyards; he got my brother into the shipyards. My father wouldn't let me go to the yards because he thought it was a dyin' trade. He wanted me to stay at school. Most of my mates left when they were fourteen. They've got all the good jobs now. Native cunnin', a lot of it.

The older people would say, "Christ! You can read and write, can't you? You can count. What the hell are you doin' in school? A laddie like you, get out and work!" So I did. I left school one Christmas when I was sixteen. I had felt like a bird in a cage. The things I was interested in, I was not bein' taught in school. Even then I had songs, I had ballads, I had stories in my head! And I wanted to learn to weave. God! I wanted to weave.

Standin' at our kitchen sink you could look into a small factory where three weavers made the warps to send out to cottage weavers. They were old people and had long since forgotten what it was to have apprentices. The machines had won over. But they were very lively people! They wouldn't have been doin' that sort of stuff if they weren't characters. They stuck to what they knew until they died. They were *strong* people. I was raised among *strong* people. Um-hmmm.

Wool is the same as people: good stuff you can do something with, and bad stuff's scarcely worth your time. In a normal fleece I can distinguish at least seven grades of wool. A hundred years ago they would have been very particular separatin' the wool because ordinary people knew quality. If they were goin' to spend money, they were goin' to get something *for* their money.

I did know people who had the equivalent of a hundred dollars in hard cash in the family. Where they had a bad landlord who wouldn't let them cultivate just a wee bit of land, they were kept very poor. Where they had better land for themselves, they could make their own shoes, make their own clothes, make their own boats, build their own houses. Sure, they had a hell of a lot of work to do, but! they weren't poverty-struck. They weren't mentally poverty-struck, either. They had all their songs and stories and a great culture behind them.

I was always tryin' to get the older people to sing the old ballads when I was young. Even if you don't understand Gaelic, the sound gets to you because it's so plaintive. They used to tell me, "Your singin's fine, but you just don't understand. Once you get your heart broken once or twice, you can start singin' heart-broken songs." Lassie, there are songs I'll never be able to sing!

Folks are always lookin' for their roots. I can't get away from mine. There's always somethin' pullin' you back. The country looks much the same here as in the highland part of Aberdeenshire. But where the hell could I start my own weavin' school at home? My mother says, "You're up in the mountains there. Couldn't you start one in your own mountains?" I said, "Ma, where could I get the money to get a piece o' ground at home?" Land costs so much more than here. The local lord still owns it. The class system is still so strong.

I've got so much more chance to do things here. Sure, there's a lot of troubles here and a lot of troubles to come, maybe, but you still can spread your wings. Och, sure, this is a good place to work and teach school.

WHEN BEA NUNZIATO BECOMES ANIMATED, *a small circle, the size of a dime, stands out slightly in the middle of her round forehead. Bea relates how she followed her husband, Rich, a Passaic, New Jersey, policeman unhappy with his job, to settle with their two children in Vermont.*

## Bea Nunziato, 36

We were on vacation in Vermont and saw an ad in the newspaper: "Chief of Police Wanted in Chester." My husband immediately drove us to this place I'd never seen before and applied. They hired him. He was the sergeant of twenty-six men in New Jersey and chief of nothing in Chester. He resigned, and we started looking for a business we could operate without any experience. There were four small stores in the village, all doing well. We figured, if they can do it, why can't we?

We looked all over the state. This store in Marshfield Village had the most potential. Hap and Irene Wells owned it. He'd had several heart attacks. Two weeks after we bought it, he had another one, so we had to learn how to operate the store on our own. People would ask for a certain item we didn't have any idea how to market. So we'd guess. I'd say to Rich, "How much do you think that's worth? He'd say, "Dollar and a quarter." I'd say, "Make it a dollar and a quarter." Or we'd say to the customer, "What did you pay for it the last time?"

Rich opens up in the morning. He puts the coffee on and brings in the bread and the newspapers. I'll get down there 9:00, 9:30, depending on how busy it is. First thing in the morning, beer salesmen will come in. We'll have a few deliveries. People at the counter don't notice you're gone, just as long as you fill up their coffee cup. Then the lunch crowd comes in. We have a lot of truck drivers. Then your people start coming home from work: groceries and beer and milk and bread. The kids want 86 pieces of penny bubble gum.

The counter keeps you busy all day. We don't do anything too difficult: hamburgers, hot dogs, bacon and eggs. I always thought, "If I can do it for my family, I can do it for anyone," until a family of six sat down at the counter — we only had six stools — and all ordered something different for breakfast.

This time of year it's very slow until fishing season opens. When the back roads start getting good, people come up to their camps for the weekend. I'll start buying Vermont plates and spoons and that kind of junk. You'd be surprised what people buy. The salesmen come in with these stupid-looking straw hats. I'll say, "My God, who's going to buy that?" They will say to me, "Y'know, Bea, just because you don't like it, doesn't mean somebody else wouldn't."

In the middle of July, when families are on vacation, we really get busy. I could never handle that pace year-round. Then comes fall foliage when you get older, retired, cranky people, mostly from out-of-state. I've got people down to a science. I can look at a person, and, without even talking to him, know exactly what he's like. A lady came up from New York City. She sat down in her fur jacket in my little store and wanted to know how old my egg salad was. I turned around and said, "Four months old." Was I insulted!

A car with a Jersey plate pulled up. My husband said to the woman, "Hi, where you from? Ah, Newark. I wouldn't live in Newark for all the tea in China." She said, "And I wouldn't live in Vermont. What have you got here? Nothing but trees and grass, trees and grass." And he said, "When was the last time you saw a tree in Newark?" She was cranky. She had that twisted look on her face when she walked in the door.

I see the local person differently than you would. I don't know how I put up with them. I have never met people as ignorant and narrow-minded as they are. They're snobs. I am here five years and feel like I moved here yesterday. Most of the women treat me like they never saw me before. If I got all dressed up in the store, God! they'd *really* hate me. I have to wear my sneakers, the old slacks and the old shirt. I have to be one of the girls. Here I am, trying to be *me*, and then I try to be *them*. It's a fraud. Most of our friends are from out-of-state because they're the only people we have anything in common with.

When we lived in Chester, they asked me if I would like to join some ladies' club. I'm not the ladies'-club type, but I thought, "To get in with the local ladies, I'll do that." This club made a reservation at a restaurant for dinner. So I got all dressed up. I had on a nice, black, two-piece suit. I wore a little jewelry and my high heels. I fixed my face up. All the women had on cotton dresses with little cardigan sweaters.

You're an out-of-stater, and they hate you for it. They think everybody from out-of-state is rich. My husband had five part-time jobs at one time. That's the only way we could save enough money to move out of New Jersey.

I'll be perfectly honest: we've made money in this store. Well, damn it! I work twelve hours a day, six and a half days a week. We're the type of person—I'm talking for my husband, too, but we're one person, our likes are so alike—who likes to see what we're working for. I say, "This store was for sale three years before I bought it. Why didn't you buy it?"

We haven't had any time off for four and a half years. Our kids are at an age where they need us more than we need the store. If anybody came in and said, "This is a nice store. I'd like to buy it," I'd say, "I'm already moved out."

BARBARA AND CHUCK BOHN LIVE *with their three children at the furthest end of Hollister Hill Road. Theirs is not one of those much-photographed, classic large white farmhouses, but a smaller version of rural solidity. Built of local brick in 1835, their home has obviously been loved into its present condition since Chuck, presently an art teacher at a local high school, bought it in 1961.*

## Barbara and Chuck Bohn, 36 and 39

BARBARA: We're both from Gary, Indiana, which is a highly industrialized town near Chicago. When Chuck was twelve, his father came out here for a workshop at Goddard College. Chuck fell in love with Vermont and later came back to paint. He was painting Mrs. Lamberton's house—the neighbor down the road—and she said, "If you like old houses, there's one down this road."

CHUCK: Which wasn't a road; it was a trail.

BARBARA: Two ruts. And he came down and found it and bought it without ever having been in it.

CHUCK: I'd seen it—

BARBARA: —Through the windows.

CHUCK: —Through the windows. I didn't come in. I always talked about coming here, but I never thought we would. Barbara started talking me into it, and then we finally just decided that—

BARBARA: We had to. If we were going to break away from our families and become people ourselves, we'd have to come here. This was really before people did their own thing. We have not had a lonesome day or a single regret. It's the best thing we ever did.

One thing I've always wanted in life, and this is snobbery on my part, is to live differently from other people. I could never see myself living in a subdivision, or playing bridge, or even being able to cope with the business of being in a neighborhood. I like other people, but this way I can have them on my own terms.

One of the first questions that everyone asks is, "How do you get out in the wintertime?" It took us two or three years of worrying in the middle of the night during a snowstorm: Would Aimard come? At the time, Aimard Lamberton ran the grader and the plow. But he always came.

We live rural, and we live at the end of a road, but one thing will never cease to amaze me: we have actually seen our tax dollars do something for us and no one else. They fixed this road for *us* once they knew we were going to stay here.

We think this is the only way to live: out in the country, here, in Vermont. Chuck is from a farm family, but I am not. I write to my friends and tell them the things that I do, and they say, "This is totally unlike what we thought you to be." But I think this is what I was meant to be. Friends visit us and say, "I wish we could live this way," but they wouldn't be willing to put the time and the work into it.

CHUCK: They think you just sit out here in the country by the fire and look out the window. They don't realize you have to cut the wood for your fire and maintain the place.

BARBARA: When we first came, we had the house to work on—and we're not really done with that—and we have the garden and our animals and sugaring and the Christmas trees.

CHUCK: We buy Christmas tree seedlings, either from a nursery or from the state, for about $30 a thousand. You put them in a slatted seed bed six-by-six until they get a good root system—at least a year. You plant them in early spring when there's still snow on the ground because they need a tremendous amount of moisture.

BARBARA: People say, "It must take you days and days to plant a thousand trees." Our system is undoubtedly not the most efficient, but we can do a couple of hundred in an hour.

CHUCK: I use a mattock, but I also made—

BARBARA: A tree-planting machine.

CHUCK: —a spade from the drive shaft of a Studebaker. It's so heavy you just throw it into the ground and push it forward and backwards and lift it out. It leaves a hole for the tree. Barbara comes along and puts the tree in and steps to seal the ground.

BARBARA: Several people have said that the tree they got from us is the prettiest tree they've ever had. They're too perfect for me. I sort of like a scraggly tree. This year we've sold five hundred to two different local groups for their money-making projects, and people come to the door. Last year we sold them for what we thought was a good price, and we had various comments.

CHUCK: Some people said I was being robbed, and some said I was getting too much, and one guy told me I would never sell them so I might as well burn them.

BARBARA: So I said, "This year we're going to write to the Christmas Tree Association of New Hampshire and Vermont and ask what we should get."

CHUCK: They told me I was doing very well, and that we mustn't get greedy because people might start buying artificial trees. We sell them for $2.00 wholesale and $3.00 to an individual buyer. You can't hurt your retailer.

BARBARA: The Christmas trees were put here as part of soil conservation. Replanting them puts our land to use. One of the reasons Vermont is so beautiful is, with all the forest, there is the contrast of the open fields.

CHUCK: But you do feel the crowd come. I know that everybody should have the right to live out in the country, but I'm afraid if everybody lived out in the country, there'd be no country for anybody to live in.

BARBARA: I feel very strongly about people being able to get out and have a little place of their own and some freedom and some seclusion, just as we do.

The longer you live here, you realize that these Vermonters are amazing people. They may be set in their ways, they may appear unsophisticated, but we have an excellent educational system, and so much of our legislation is unbelievably progressive. It comes from people who aren't going to be told what to do, from people who take their good time about something. I know we'll never be considered Vermonters, but maybe, some day, some of our descendents will.

CHUCK STANDER CONFESSES *that "both my wife and I quit our jobs and came here without any idea of what we were going to do." Inspired by a book, Hermann Hesse's* Narcissus and Goldmund, *Chuck opened a woodworking shop in Marshfield Village. Now he lives in a mostly renovated house on Beaver Meadow Road with his wife, Pat, and their young daughter.*

## Chuck Stander, 29

I taught philosophy for four years at a small liberal-arts college in Baltimore. Like, we had tried living in a commune of professional people. We didn't want to move back into apartment or suburban life. We thought we'd get enough land to explore different social and physical environments.

In Baltimore, to go further south is to be in the South. In your rural areas people feel like they're at a dead end. Anything new doesn't fit in with the mentality. It destroys a pathos of, like, being in a decline. They live off of that as much as they suffer from it.

We started looking in New York State. I didn't find it much better. I hate to use such an inaccurate word as "vibes," but it's a question of there being a climate of, like, friendliness, at least surface friendliness — at least no hostility. Vermonters are a little cool, yet there's not the feeling, "You're intruding on my game plan."

We settled here for several reasons. I didn't want to be too far away from colleges. Being rather insecure as to what I was going to do, I thought I could always fall back on my degree as a way of making money. Because of the number of young people like us up here, you would have a readily identifiable group that would be your social peers.

How do you reintegrate work and your social lifestyle? Small communities based upon small businesses. Vermont discourages both big business and big farming. It's probably the only way to get around, like, the dead ends that the cities are running into. Dispersing people and business becomes much more possible as the Industrial Revolution, which made everything come together in big cities, peters out, and the technological one takes over.

Before I came here, I didn't believe that I could do anything with my hands. I lived on a farm, but my dad wouldn't let me work on the machinery or do anything that took skill. I always hired people to do whatever it was that I wanted done. The first thing we did when we got up here was work on the house.

Putting on a new roof entailed a big switch in mentality. We read the back of the shingle box and did it. Then we built the addition, which was, like, the biggest mental barrier I've ever overcome. We read through a government pamphlet on wood-frame structures, which didn't make any sense. So we'd read a chapter and go out and do it and come in and read the next chapter. Sure enough, the whole thing kind of grew up. It made you believe that you could do anything.

About a month later I had the possibility of taking this job with the Social Welfare Department. But the idea of working with wood grew in my mind. I thought, "For once in your life, like, go ahead and pursue your fantasy." So the husband of the other couple that moved up with us and I got the shop. Neither one of us had done any kind of woodworking beyond making a bookcase. Neither one of us had ever run a business. He was an English major; I was a philosophy major. We learned woodworking from talking to old-timers, and trial and error.

We started our furniture-making career making pine furniture. Pine was readily available and the cheapest. Now we're trying to work solely in native woods: mostly butternut, cherry, maple, birch, a little beech and basswood and oak. I'm wholesaling contemporary furniture down in New York now. I don't see it as necessary that I should make my living within the locality. I see handcraft as one of Vermont's most significant exports.

As long as the satisfaction of working with wood keeps expanding, I'll pursue it. If it got to the point where the only market was mass production, it would take out the creativity and pleasure. Since there isn't that much money in it—if we sold everything we made, my take-home pay could conceivably reach $6,000—there wouldn't be any reason to stay.

The other reason I'd leave would be disenchantment. The guy that used to be my partner always said that Vermont seemed to smile on you for a moment, and then kick you in the ass. Everything that you seem to accomplish, you pay dearly for. Because of the climate you cannot make a lot of mistakes. When you're experimenting, where mistakes are part of the game, you end up losing something for everything that you gain.

My wife and I started this whole thing at about the same time that we started our family. The impact of, like, switching lifestyles, starting a family and starting a business was incredibly hard. It really puts a strain on you and your relationship to other people. Vermont seems to have a very high divorce rate. Everybody I know was once married.

Plus, you're working at a kind of '60's mentality: the Kennedy era of optimism that you could really make a better society. The concept of self-actualization and authenticity became part of what people wanted out of life. It isn't just talk anymore. It is experienced as a need. A fairly foreign place—this rural society with its built-in climatic challenges—is sometimes painful to be in.

I've experienced, like, different energy cycles that follow the seasons here. Summertime is an incredible beehive of energy. Everybody is going a mile a minute because there's so much you've saved up to do. They know that, when it's June, winter is really not that far off. I have yet to live comfortably with feeling that cold weather is just around the corner when it's not even warm yet.

In the wintertime, like, the pace of life more than halves. Everybody's adrenaline concentrates on keeping warm. I have a love-hate thing going with the winter—mostly hate. I have not yet made my peace with the cold. Most of the people I know haven't. Around February, everybody is going through some kind of minor mental breakdown.

AN ISRAELI BORN IN JERUSALEM, *Noga Trevès Langfur came to this country in 1973. Because her husband, Stephen, had previously attended Goddard College, they were interested in living in the area. They are house-mates of Kirk Gardner, who lives up the road. While Stephen works on his Ph.D., Noga writes and studies dance.*

## Noga Langfur, 25

Did I tell you about my grandfather? It's an unusual story. I'm of Spanish descent: Ladino-speaking Jews. Ladino is an ancient Spanish dialect that the Jews who were expelled from Spain in 1492 took with them. My father's family then went to France and settled in Alsace-Lorraine in a town called Trèves. That's my maiden name. Alsace-Lorraine was a region where Germans and French quarreled, so my family went to Italy.

In Italy they were for many generations, from the sixteenth century up to the nineteenth century. There were many rabbis among them. They were really people of the book because they had a printing house. My grandfather found himself in Turkey and then moved to Syria. He was a manager of the railway during the Turkish Empire. At one point the Turks massacred the Armenians viciously. As the railway manager, he used to "lose" wagons of wheat and save many Armenians from starvation.

He is a true Zionist because in his twenties he had this longing to go to Jerusalem. He was not involved with any political group. He had this basic feeling of a Jew: *Jerusalem.* Unlike the European Jew that packed and left, mostly under persecution, he packed and left out of his own will. He went to the other place. Since then we are there.

That ties in with your question: Do you feel that you have displaced other people? We were there. There is a continuity. The Jews that live in the Arab countries — the Oriental Jews — are proof of being inherent in the region. But the clash between the Jews and the Palestinians is quite tragic because we cannot afford to lose, and they have nothing to lose, so they are desperate.

I see a similarity between Oriental Jews and Palestinians. They look alike, Semites. They both emphasize the intellect. Being displaced is exile. Palestinians became the Jews of the Jews. It's certain that we both have a claim for this land. What to do about a solution is a different matter. This situation is full of ironies.

The years between '67 and this last war were years of short-sightedness, I would call it, because we didn't do enough to meet the Palestinians. We could have made the first gesture, and we didn't. When I say, "We didn't," I mean the official government. Individuals did. I was part of a group who wanted to know each other better culturally. There were Palestinians and Israelis, but it was also a stage for other minority groups: Ethiopians, Armenians, Karaim, Shomronim, Baha'is. Because we felt that Jerusalem is a special city, we wanted to talk with each other.

Jerusalem is a holy city because of the alleys that are winding. "Alleys," you say? Because of the marketplaces in the open air, because of the stones. The whole city is built on stones. Although you see scenes of everyday, there is a special quality in twilight and radiation of the stones. There is weight because of the paradoxes, because of the mosques and the churches and the synagogues. The people go with bright eyes when they walk in Jerusalem. They feel: I am in the center of the world.

I don't miss Jerusalem because there is always a longing to be in another place. Thinking about me being here on Hollister Hill, I feel: this is the other place. It has a certain magic: deer, squirrels, snow. Especially the meeting with a deer. This is something I can't get over. Vermont is like a legend. When I was small, I used to read Grimms' stories. Because the sun was scorching, I never understood them, really. Suddenly, I'm here. This is the world, the world is one. This place is more time because you see the changing of the seasons. I don't feel estranged, but I am not in my element.

I'm looking forward to the rest of the winter here. It's because I like extremes. I've been in the desert of Sinai for three years. It was very clean landscape. There was sunrise and sunset and people. In the desert, people were the trees, were the bushes, the roads, the colors. In the winter, here, the landscape is people.

ALTHOUGH RESIDENTS OF A HILL *do not belong to a neighborhood, as traditionally defined, living along sparsely settled back roads inclines one towards interdependence. We are reluctant to quarrel with a neighbor who pulls the car out of a ditch during an ice storm, or with the woman down the road who fills water jugs from her tap when the pipes freeze. While friendship, enmity or romance may develop with those living nearby, it is neighborliness that sustains us.*

*Kirk Gardner, who lives at "the four corners" towards the upper end of the hill, worked as a broadcast journalist in New York City and Philadelphia. Formerly the Director of Media at Goddard College, Kirk and his housemates often cross-country ski on the snowmobile trails behind the houses and across the fields.*

## Kirk Gardner, 32

I first came to Vermont because I wanted to learn how to ski. I spent a year over in the Mad River Valley. Downhill skiing is a lot of fun, but it's also expensive and a little hollow. It's very individualistic — yourself set against nature, snow, the mountains — but you develop an implicit kind of competitiveness. It permeates everything you do: how you dress, where you live, what you drive, the time you get up, where you go at night, and what you do when you get there.

You live with some pretty high-living folks. You've got to deal with

their sets of values, their perceptions about the world, their sense of how to relate to each other and to themselves. If I can generalize unfairly, it tends to involve a lack of personal perception. It comes because it's not highly valued to be in touch with anything other than the mechanical existence of your life. You're bussed up to the slope in a rather fancy car; you're towed up the hill in an expensive electrical tow; you're kept in fancy surroundings. All of which is very reflective, despite the fact it's considered rustic and rural, of technological America, 1974.

One of the difficult results of this is that you've taken what was at one time probably the most beautiful valley in the state and turned it into a little bit of honky-tonk. There's been an economic impact on this region, not only in terms of the environment, but also on the people who live there. There was a tremendous economic depression in the state. The ski industry augmented — and, still, I think, has the possibility of successfully augmenting — what was then a meager economy. People suddenly found their land, that had been literally worthless at ninety cents an acre, was all of a sudden worth something — up to $100, $200 an acre.

But they found themselves in an awkward position. As the area was developed, their taxes were going up, yet their cash income was not. People who had lived there all their lives began to sell out to people who used the place for a part-time residence. There are two dairy farmers left in Warren, a town which was all dairy farms fifteen years ago.

That changed the whole economic basis of the Valley. You end up with a very definite division in the classes of people who live there. There are those who are clearly among the American aristocracy. These are the moneyed, outside vacationers, some of whom are part-time residents, who come in to enjoy the leisure of the Valley. They pay a reasonable amount of taxes, but also derive a substantial amount of service. There's not a native among them, I dare say.

Then there's the slave class, the ski bums — "snow niggers" is the word — who are held in a very low opinion by both natives and by outside people. They are mostly college kids who want to ski but can't afford it. They make a living by making beds and washing dishes and slinging hash, working the tows or shoveling snow. They get room and board, tips, whatever you can wangle for cash out of anybody you have a hustle with, and a season's pass. The season's pass is what they're working for.

The third class is the native Vermonters, some of whom have managed to stay. They are gas-station owners, lodge owners who shifted over from farming, people who run a skimobile dealership. Those people are caught in the middle. In numbers they are almost a minority now. I would guess that as much as a half to three-fourths of the physical work is done by people who were born and raised in the state, for which they receive a good bit less than a half of the goods that are floating around.

That's my perception of the problems in the Valley. You get out because you are equally appalled by what happened there as you were by what happened in New York and New Jersey. I merely found myself living in a rural New Jersey. Cross-country skiing seems to offer a way out. It doesn't destroy the environment. It's not confined to one area. In spreading it out, you can diffuse some of the more pernicious aspects of a sport which develops a certain amount of elitism.

One of the joys of cross-country skiing is that you can extend substantially the area which you identify with on foot. It gives you the same kind of pleasure that you get out of downhill skiing—control, sense of identity with nature, sense of challenge from the mountain, from the snow—but the time, the place, the pleasure and the tranquillity to begin to think about who you are, what's going on around you, what the world is made up of, and what your place in it is.

We've got to make a decision over something very simple: to what extent will we cross-country skiers utilize the snow-machine trails around here? Snow-machine trails are nifty to ski on: they are already packed, they generally connect groups of people, they generally go in the straightest path, and they often go through some of the prettiest terrain. If we set up parallel, separate trails, we're going to end up producing an elitist way of getting around.

A large number of local Vermonters see that their values are being challenged. They're likely to be obliterated by us, the more cosmopolitan people who've come into the state. We both stand to lose a considerable amount, collectively as a community, if we let one side obliterate the other. We've got to forge a bridge across that gap. If we don't, we're going to be headed for all kinds of serious problems between people who have a substantially different set of values and no way to talk about the differences. One of the great strengths of Vermont is its tremendous capacity to tolerate differences. We've got to find ways in which we can marry these two cultures.

FROM THEIR HOUSE *at the foot of the hill, across the road from a federally subsidized apartment project, Bill and Corinne Smith have watched the steady in-migration of, mostly, city people. "I don't know of any place on the face of the planet Earth that I would choose to migrate to. If we could find an*

*inexpensive way within our means to get to an inhabitable planet, I would*
*take the boys and then send for my wife." Bill Smith's image echoes, of*
*course, the historical reality of Vermont's white settlement. But there is little*
*remaining unsettled land in northern New England. There is merely the*
*restless influx of new people.*

## Bill and Corinne Smith, 49 and 43

BILL: I would like to reduce the population in the state of Vermont
back down to about 250,000. I believe that the growth of the population here reflects the population explosion out of the urban centers.
What they sought was the bucolic loveliness of the place. That which
they came to find, they destroyed by coming here. I'm expressing dis-
satisfaction with the fact that I have so many people around here. That
has probably long been the complaint of anybody that was there
before somebody else.

I don't understand how accurate hearsay is in this particular case,
but I understand people come here for temporary jobs. If they don't
have enough money, they go down and apply for relief in the form of
food stamps or welfare. I can't understand people that would put
themselves in a position of having to accept aid in a place they were
going to, when, perhaps, they didn't need it where they came from.

The people I really can't understand up here are not those of you
that have children and are raising them, but those that come here and
do not have children. Or come here with a lifestyle that very definitely
will not produce any children. They abnegate the true responsibilities
of an adult. I don't accept their statement that our population has to
achieve a certain level. If population control were the only route, several of the aborigines here would have been blowing up bridges on the
interstate.

I am one of the aborigines. I don't feel displaced. I was born here,
my wife was born here, my children were born here, my mother was
born here, my father was born here, my wife's mother was born here,

my wife's father was born here. When they talk about the Vermont regiments that flanked Pickett's charge in the Battle of Gettysburg, they were relatives of mine. This is where my people are.

I would hope my sons and daughters wouldn't be faced with this continuing annoyance of all these people wanting to come here. There is no way under the federal constitution for us to deny anybody to come here at any time they wish. At the same time you cannot take away the property rights that are also guaranteed.

CORINNE: I was born and brought up twenty miles from here. And I've lived here for, what? going on ten years, and I'm still a foreigner.

BILL: Dear, that's my fault. The day that I told these people over here I had no interest in joining the Masons, I had no interest in the fire department —

CORINNE: It's a cold town.

BILL: No, it isn't, dear.

CORINNE: It's a cold town. Most Vermont towns are.

ORIGINALLY FROM BOSTON, *Jules Rabin, with his wife, Helen, came to Vermont after living in New York City. Educated at Harvard, he teaches anthropology at Goddard College. He and Helen, with their two young daughters, live midway on the hill between their two neighbors, Kirk Gardner and Bill Smith.*

## Jules Rabin, 49

Americans have chosen what I've come to call a Daniel Boone existence. If you've got 200 acres, you put your cabin in the middle. I have inclinations in that direction. I wish that, instead of these measly little

five acres, I had 200. Still, it's a misbegotten ideal to have land separating you from other folk. There is more social connective tissue
developing on Hollister Hill between ourselves — the newcomers —
and the natives. But we'll never make it. We have a kind of sickness of
human isolation. We don't have what so-called savage people have: a
good, daily integration with other folk. Socializing in the American
sphere means having dinner with friends or dropping over for coffee.
The remote ideal that I have in mind is where people are engaged with
each other in multiple ways. They work together.

I've learned a kind of pragmatic inclination to be courteous here.
The person whom you're discourteous to today is going to show up in
some significant relationship next month or next year. A few mornings ago I went to the Goddard College Library. It was maybe 8:32.
The doors were closed. They're supposed to be open at 8:30. I rapped
a little, then quickly got New York-style impatient and began rapping
loudly. It's always a stranger who opens the door to you in New York.

Who should come along but a maintenance woman. We've had a
growing familiarity and regard for each other. I was mortified. I put
my hand to my face. I fumbled some apology. A couple of mornings
previously I had a long talk with this woman about the state of things
locally. She had been a country woman when she grew up. The native
people got sold a terrible bill of goods by the electric corporations and
the supermarkets that they could live like the fancy city people.

This woman, as with other people, is turning towards more self-
sufficiency, more decentralization. In good part, it's economics. But
there's also a nostalgia developing. People are saying, "There's nothing
like wood heat." Maybe it's a delusion. If so, people's delusions are
going in that direction. Here I was, seven years in Vermont, giving her
information about wood heating systems. I find it very strange that we
late-comers picked up, quickly and superficially, some of the old
information, so that we're able to return it to native people.

Although I probably never was a real deep-down New Yorker, I
have some regrets about leaving the city. The city is the apex of civili-

zation. We miss things here. It's as though we've cut out a large sector of what has been a-building for 2,000 years. But something has been developing here that makes this region richer than New York. It's almost like a piece of Darwinian evolution. While New York is faltering, we here are building up something else. It's pretty piddling now, to be sure, but on the scale of who we are and what we were doing in the years before the present, there are some good things developing here.

I'm not a visionary man, but I have visions of the kids going on and living here. At the same time, and this is significant (I haven't expressed it to myself or to anybody), I feel it's small potatoes up here. There's no preeminence, no glamour. It's just plain folks, plain living. Maybe it's Jewish ambition, but something in me, old-fashioned and unreconstructed, thinks of my kids doing high-falutin' things. You need an audience of a million, not of eighty like you get around Marshfield and Plainfield. That's in conflict with what I'm living by, and with anthropological ideals, where to be integrated with your community is the chief goodness of life.

THIS INTERVIEW WITH PAUL BOUCHARD *took place one winter evening in the Bouchards' plain, squarish farmhouse on East Hill Road in East Calais. A complex person with a strong, clear intelligence, Paul never answered a question until he'd thought about it. No rush, but no slowness, either. This man's primary question, based on his declining physical strength, was whether he could afford farming his 230 acres.*

## Paul Bouchard, 35

Everything about this winter is different: we sold the cows this fall.

My back had been bothering me real bad for two years. Last summer, three hours of cropping—seeding down our fields and doing our haying—were the most I could stand and still be able to milk my cows night and morning. As the summer progressed, the doctor finally said, "If you don't make a drastic change, you will probably be infirm."

I had an infinite variety of things to go into. I had done some business with this company that worked with farmers and agriculture. They were looking for dealers. I wouldn't commit myself to call on my friends and my neighbors until I knew more about them. Around the first of December, I did go to work for them.

Besides that, I still have sixty heifers I'm taking care of. I've got twenty-five animals that belong to other fellows besides my own. There's quite a number of farmers that would like to do this, but they are very reluctant to turn their animals over into somebody else's care. I guess my reputation was so that they weren't afraid to leave their animals.

I was born on a dairy farm about thirty miles from here. I worked for my dad after I was married. I had three brothers and there was plenty of help at home, so we decided to go into it on our own. Three years after we came, we had to either build a new barn or discontinue farming here. We chose to build a new barn. But instead of having twenty-five cows, this meant we had to keep a minimum of forty because of the extra payments. All this tended to cause the farm to keep growing and growing.

For me to just stay here is very expensive. But anyone with less than $100,000 for the down payment can't buy this farm. Plus, they've got to replace all the animals we sold. The payments will be so high that it's very marginal. But if I sell this farm, I'm also probably selling any chance our boys will ever have of farming. And this leaves me in a predicament if we're working to do what's best for the entire family.

I can remember my grandfather relating transactions he made when he started farming. He came from Canada around 1916. All he had was a team of horses. He bought a small farm from a farmer. He gave him all the money he had. The balance was usually carried by the owner. Every spare dollar was put towards paying this balance within a year or two. It was almost like an obsession. That's much different from our philosophy towards borrowing and spending.

You quite often have to hear the older people talk about the hard times they had. But when we sit down with a pencil and paper and

start doing some figuring, their margins for profit were greater than ours are today. Their volume was much smaller, so the money they had was not much. Technology was basically experience. They didn't rely so much on universities and studies in farm magazines. It was a matter of knowing what worked on your farm. You visited with your neighbors, and you found out what they did that worked.

Different fellows working here have observed that something tells me when to do what. I don't try to explain it; I don't even try to understand it. I just know that it works. I had a very casual way of knowing when the weather was right. The percent of hay that went in the barn without getting wet was very favorable. I wasn't aware of this until someone made a joke one day. This fellow was telling his father, "He's got somebody telling him when the weather's going to be good." Until that day I figured everybody used this same method. I can do this with animals, too. Does it boil down to a sensitivity towards certain things?

I spent a lot of time around my grandfather, more than I ever did with my father. He had the time to get me to observe things I would have missed my whole life. When I was a little kid, the idea of riding to the fields was out. We walked. I would always be tagging along.

And while we were walking, he would point out the way the birds were flying. He would say, "It's going to rain" within so many hours. And I'd say, "How can you tell?" "Oh," he says, "you watch the way those birds over there are flying. Tomorrow you watch and see how those birds are flying." I would pay attention. They didn't fly the same at all.

After I got out of school and came up here, I started being more sensitive to everything. When we were going through school, we hardened to certain things, at least in the environment I was in. Kids can be cruel towards each other. They'll make fun of peculiarities or uniquenesses, rather than encouraging them. They're ridiculed. They build walls. I think if a person reaches a point where he can or she can feel somewhat secure, they can reverse the thing and develop sensitivities towards their whole environment.

I've sure gotten off the subject of farming, but this is where I live now. The kind of books I read and the kind of discussions I like to get into are very much related to psychic phenomena. Anything that will go beyond material things holds a real interest for me.

A NATIVE OF VERMONT, *Louise Bouchard grew up primarily in Barre, where her father worked in the granite sheds. Married to Paul Bouchard, she cares for a large house, along with four children; she also helps in the barn when her husband is unable to work alone. Our conversation was squeezed in between Louise's vacuuming the living room and feeding the baby.*

## Louise Bouchard, 36

Right now our daily routine is so different. I've always helped in the barn, besides the housework. With this new job, sometimes Paul's here and sometimes he's not. It makes your household very unorganized, shall I say?

If he's sitting in there reading, I'd rather sit and do nothing, too. It's been plaguing me. Maybe it's jealousy that he's doing nothing and I still have my kids to take care of? Meals to get? It's something you don't feel good about.

Right now it's a slack time, but when spring comes, it's going to be altogether different. This is when he has to sell his product. Plus, he has the farm, still, so he's got the spring work to do. I'll probably be complaining that I don't see anything of him then. I think you hear women complaining more than men.

It's not that I'm envious of him being out. I don't care about working outside. I'm satisfied to be a housekeeper, or "homemaker," I guess they call it today. A woman belongs at home with her little ones. If she's there, they turn out better.

I don't go for women's lib. I believe that a woman is treated more like a lady if she acts like one, rather than trying to be one of the guys. Yet, there are some women that would rather be working in an office.

We were married, what, six, seven years before we had our oldest one. My life changed completely. I had worked out for an insurance company and helped my husband on weekends and in the evening. After I had the children, this became my total environment.

You hear of other women saying that they go off for an afternoon, but I don't feel that I can take the time. I have to do my washing and cooking and ironing before I can sit down to sew or go visiting. That's the way I was brought up. Mother always was at home and did these things. To be outside was second place.

You aren't free to be yourself. I don't know if that's exactly what I mean. It's a wrong attitude, I tell you, because I don't think that I should come first. But I should have a time when I can do what I want.

We've lived here for almost fourteen years. I've always enjoyed the fact that I've helped with the farm. But Paul is the provider. Where he feels we should go, I'm satisfied. I'll get used to the change.

# *Spring*

ALTHOUGH SNOW OFTEN STAYS ON THE GROUND until the middle of April, March signals the quickening of the northern year. Its first sign is a desperate spider imprisoned in the bathtub. A day or two later a southeast wind confirms the possibility of change. This is the treacherous time of spring hope and of winter reality — a small warmth at noon followed by arctic winds in the middle of the night. Impatient with the routine caution of winter, we long for the first days of increasing light and diminishing snow.

Tourists who come only to stare at fall foliage miss the subtle, important rising of the color in the trees in early spring. Every trunk is distinct, the light almost visibly separating the shiny poplar, chalky white birch, smooth-skinned beech, and dependable maple.

In the growing light, dogs start to shed. Mouse droppings appear in a bottom kitchen drawer. A skunk hurries across the road. One morning a hundred blackbirds alight on a farmer's field. The most undemonstrative of citizens (face radiant) declares, "Now, I know you've already seen your first robin," anticipating that the smug neighbor will reply, "Oh, yes, at least a week ago when I was down to Montpelier." A storm predictably arrives the next day.

The sudden melting of late snows in early April pulls winter's frost out of the roads, causing Vermont's fifth season — mud season. Snow goes, grass grows — almost immediately. The upland fields gradually become the faint green of old-fashioned, hand-tinted postcards. The spring light quietly burrows into even the shaded woods. After several warming days, a late-afternoon shower approaches from the east. The water rushes off pastures and slopes, through culverts, across fields, until it reaches the high rivers. Rain becomes wet snow; snow turns to rain. A hard, spitting snow — "poor-man's fertilizer" — deposits minerals on untilled fields and gardens.

Because this is the only time of year that foundations aren't hidden by snow, grass or fallen leaves, you can see where the skeletons of houses and barns, fences and trees adjoin the muscular earth. Farmhouses with attached ells and barns are visibly connected like a problem in long division. With spring begins the emergence of old people from closed houses. A thickly built woman stands with fists on her waist, surveying a future tulip bed. A rake supports a man's left hand while he gossips with a neighbor. While girls jump rope, boys play with toy trucks in the driveway.

Spring fever reaches epidemic proportions when daylight saving begins in April. Although there is still the possibility of cold rains or a brief snow, by May the earth smells like a living animal. The ponds glitter; it hurts your eyes to look directly at green fields at noon. Asparagus grows the way children draw all living things — straight up from the ground. Lilac blossoms sit in a jar on the kitchen table.

The cattle look stunned as they're let out of the barn onto pasture. Abandoning their sunny porches, dogs look for shade. Deer retreat from fields to the woods, except for late at night. Over the ridge a thin fox disappears. Black flies swarm the second week of May, followed by mosquitoes and deer flies.

All kinds of vehicles go up and down the freshly graded roads every sunny day. Gardeners bend towards the turned-over soil as pea fences go up. Along the river, gulls follow a cultivator opening the earth. At dusk a family picks stones from a future cornfield before the moving tractor. The noise of lawnmowers replaces that of chainsaws and snow machines.

A local newspaper, *The Times Argus*, notes:

Six stalwart men of the congregation spent Saturday afternoon transplanting 20-foot trees to beautify the church landscape. Under the supervision of plantsman Phil Hodgdon, Pete Trask, Bill Abbott and Wes Herwig set out three maples and one oak beside the 1791 meetinghouse, and moved one maple near the parsonage. Rhubarb pie and lemonade were served to the workers by Mrs. Herwig.

There are more modest labors. "Do you have plans for spring?" I asked Viiu Lincoln, who lives towards the bottom of the hill. "Yes, I do," she said, "I have plans for opening up every window in the house."

ROBERT SCHWARTZ, WHO WORKS FOR THE VERMONT *Transportation Agency, is moderator of Marshfield's Town Meeting, held the first Tuesday in March in the high school auditorium. While the political and financial direction of local government is discussed with seriousness, townspeople also have an opportunity to catch up on gossip and evaluate how well their neighbors have endured the winter.*

## Robert Schwartz, 48

This was my third year as Moderator. Unless you foul up terribly, people seem to like to leave you in there. The only shortcoming is it precludes sounding off too much. The Moderator only works one day of the year, but he does have absolute control. He has to be careful and not let his own biases show, because, under the Vermont Statutes, there's really no one who can question a Moderator's ruling.

Maybe this goes back to earlier days when all our politics tended to get a little more violent. If you had an issue that was pretty emotional, someone had to be able to quiet it down long enough to actually hold your meeting. People used to be more directly affected by the things done in the town than they were on the state or national scale. Maybe as a nation we aren't, but as individuals we seem to be less prone to settle our problems with physical violence.

I personally hope we continue to have the type of balloting and election of officers that we have now, right at the meeting itself. It keeps people more interested in local government. When we lose this, we've lost an awful lot. All the way from state government down, this is one of the beauties of Vermont: that government is close to the people. In what other state can John Q. Citizen, who has a problem or a question, or is just nosy, walk in and see the governor? You can do that here. There's not the sixteen dozen assistants and the assistants to the assistants that screen out most people.

The participation of people in their government, to me, makes Vermont a wonderful place to live. Up here, because of the smallness and because of the form of government, anyone that's lived here any time at all quickly finds out that they can be busy every night of the week. We have a lot of new people—I mean they've been here maybe five years—that are taking an interest in town affairs. I think in many cases this is why they come in; they want to get involved in their community's activities. But we have some people who come in who merely want to change everything. Their approach is: "I know more than you do, and you'd better listen to me." This is going to turn anybody off.

I think that most Vermonters (I've found it so; I was a newcomer) accept people on their face value. It's not whether they're new or whether they've been in Vermont all their life; they are taken on what they are as a person. If they don't like them, they ignore them. If they like them—if they're an acceptable kind of person in their eyes—why, then they are accepted.

Taking Hollister Hill as a little corner of Marshfield, I don't think you can say that there is any one kind of philosophy or ideology or anything else up here, even amongst the long-time families. You have the same thing in newcomers—people of all kinds. They all seem to mix pretty well and get involved in community affairs. They don't always agree, but it would be a terrible place to live if everybody agreed all the time—especially if you're a Town Moderator. Town meetings would be very dull.

ALTHOUGH THE TAXPAYER *pays the greatest sum to the federal government, the local town and school budgets are the only ones over which he or she has any say. Thus, elections of members to the school board during town meeting reflect the community's divisions. At the time of her interview, Ellen Pitkin, a daughter-in-law of Tim and Helen Pitkin, had recently been elected to the twelve-member Twinfield School Board. Although surprised by her success, "newer" people considered her election a triumph of their point of view. Ellen is also involved with Plainfield Little Theater, which began in the 1930's and currently attracts amateur actors and theater-goers.*

## Ellen Pitkin, 41

I was born in Kentucky. My father came to Goddard College in 1944 when I was ten years old. While I was in high school, I knew everybody in Plainfield. You could drive through the town and say, "So-and-so lives there." Now I have no idea who people are. When you live out on a hill place, you get a different perspective. I don't know how much I feel a part of the community, except for the school and the community theater.

The whole community is very proud of the school and of the kids. People care about giving their kids the best chance they can. It's just a matter of how. They see me as a radical, and I'm not. I don't even know if I fall into the category of "liberal." What you want is balanced representation. At the moment, it's not. The "other" side is the older community, the non-Goddard-oriented community. It's the people who are afraid of change or don't understand what the change means. They live in a local community, protecting local rights.

Some people don't make an effort to be a part of the local community. I'll cite the New School group as an example. They wanted a better education for their kids. In their withdrawal from the community, they became an elitist group. One woman said to me, "My child will never have to deal with anybody who's not a college graduate, so why should I send him to the public school?" This attitude is of no use to me. The most important thing you can learn in school is how to work cooperatively with different types of people.

In a rural community you have more opportunities to get involved simply because there are not many people. I don't know if I would have gotten involved in the community theater group otherwise. I've always loved going to the theater. I was in high-school plays because there were only three girls in my class. I've even been known to watch the soaps for a little drama.

Last summer we did Shaw's *Arms and the Man*. There were only eight of us in the play, but we got people coming out of the woods who were interested in theater. It brought in different elements of the community. Our next major accomplishment was doing Gilbert and Sullivan's *The Yeoman of the Guard* through the flu season, the bad winter driving and the basketball season. We still had to turn people away. We can only hold 150 in the Plainfield Town Hall.

We chose the Town Hall because it has a nice feeling. The size, the acoustics, the relationship between the players and the audience, the sentimentality of tradition are perfect. But it's got technical problems. There are no backstage facilities of any kind. You go out of the backstage window to the house next door if you have to go to the bathroom. We use the balcony as a dressing room. We have to borrow lighting.

Still, I like living here. I love this house. I spend a lot of time looking out the window. I do like the people and the size of the community. I don't mind the school. The state is beautiful. You can exist in one pair of blue jeans, no matter where you go — even the Governor's office — and not feel like a freak. I don't think you could find another place to live that would give you as much.

SINCE NO SMALL TOWN IN VERMONT *can afford to pay salaried fire fighters, each community has a volunteer force. In addition to frequent training sessions, volunteer fire fighters must leave whatever they're doing the instant the fire siren sounds. Fire fighter Tinker Codling, who lives towards the bottom of the hill with his wife, Ellen, and three teenaged children, works as a plumber for a local septic-system and plumbing firm.*

## Tinker Codling, 38

The Fire Chief asked me to join the Plainfield Volunteer Fire Department in '62. They were short of men. I could see where it was somethin' that benefited the community.

Firemen and departments have come a long ways in the last ten years. With volunteer work we remodeled the old gym into a fire station. The equipment is more modern. Property damage has been much less. Most of the towns in the surrounding area belong to Mutual Aid, so there's always a backup.

Plainfield had only three fires this winter. One was a toaster, which was out when we got there. Another was an overheated stovepipe. The people had it out by the time we got there. A chair was burnin' at Goddard College, but they have a very good Fire Department. We never did get there.

Chimney fires and electricity are major causes of fires. We've had some start from gasoline. Up on Maple Hill a guy had a frozen toilet. He dumped gasoline in and lit it. He thought he was goin' to thaw out his sewer line. It blew the toilet up. That wasn't using common sense, as far as I'm concerned.

We have five fire phones in town. As one of the Assistant Fire Chiefs, I have one. It is hitched into the siren in the village. If we was settin' here and the fire phone rang, I'd answer it. I'd head for the fire station to see that our truck is out and our tanker's out. If none of that equipment's left, I usually take the pumper. Then we proceed to the fire.

When I get to a fire, I try to find somebody that can give a head count of the people livin' in the building. Sometimes it's hard to identify the owner. There's more strange people comin' into the area that aren't the native people you have grown up with. There's a lot of new names and faces. If they mention, "The place used to be so-and-so's," we're all set.

You size up what you need for lines so you can hit with the best advantage and use the least amount of water. If it's a fire in your own town, you stay until it's safe to leave. Sometimes it's fifteen minutes, sometimes it's four or five hours before you come back home. When you get back, you clean all your equipment and trucks and replace what you've used. The new hose today don't need to be dried, but if it was older hose, which we do have, you have to hang it up and let it dry.

We had a major grass fire one Sunday last spring. Because people were givin' a description of the same fire at different locations, we had all our equipment out of the station goin' different ways. It was such a hot fire it took most of the equipment to save the house. We couldn't save the barn. It was so muddy that we couldn't get the equipment to the pond. We were settin' up portable pumps. The grass was catchin' afire and goin' into the woods. They had a sawmill up in the pasture that burned.

We've had two deaths since I've been on the Department. A woman was lightin' a wood fire with kerosene. It blew up and caught her clothes on fire. It was all over before the Fire Department was even called. A girl was burned to death in Plainfield. It was caused by an overheated stovepipe. The building was so much in flames that nobody could get in. It was 25 to 30 degrees below zero. We left here around three o'clock in the mornin', and it was five o'clock at night before I came home.

We like every man to know all the jobs. There's a few that can't wear an air pack, but maybe they're good at runnin' the pumper or drivin' the tank truck. Some men don't want to climb on a roof. I run the pumper, I work with a mask, I climb, but I'm a little older than when I first joined. A half-hour of fightin' fire steady, and I'm ready to step back. The next day I'm so lame I can hardly walk.

We usually have around eighteen to twenty men in the Department. You'd like to get the young fellows in because they've got more endurance, but they leave town. The same fellows that have been on for ten, twelve, fifteen years are still here.

THE MAILMAN, *a federal employee of the Plainfield Post Office, works six days out of seven. He has gone halfway around his route by 9:30 in the morning, which is when the mail is delivered to my box. As it would have been against government regulations for me to accompany a rural carrier on his mail route, I met Bob Morse one April afternoon after work to reenact his daily ride over Hollister Hill.*

## Bob Morse, 48

The postal service claims that one of the best ways to handle mail is through a rural free delivery service. All the customer pays for is his mailbox. Rural carriers pride themselves on a little bit of service. In order to supply this service, the customer must make the effort to erect his mailbox and keep the approach to the box cleared out.

I've got 313 boxes, and if everybody didn't shovel their box out during the winter, you can imagine what the day would be like. Even though postal regulations say if the box isn't plowed out, you don't have to leave the mail, you usually make an effort. If they don't make the effort, you just drive by. That usually will straighten it right out.

In the post office we have what we call a "case," which actually is a pigeonhole for every person on the route. You draw the mail out backwards so it comes off the way you're traveling. You put as much as you can in a bundle and put a strap around it to carry it.

I put this strap of mail right on the seat; I put the small packages down in front on the passenger side where your feet would be, and the big ones I put over in back of me. I can carry some of this so-called junk mail here over the drive shaft. You cuss a little bit if you have two or three box-stuffers all the same day; other than that you don't give it any thought.

You don't want to forget anything, and normally you won't, but when you get all these box-stuffers, and you get your eyes to going every which way, you may. See, you're watching your boxholders, so you're going to drive by a mailbox and forget to leave a package. This is the thing that's most common to forget.

There's no real art to putting mail in. You get to the point where you can reach in and drop the mail and grab the letters that are there all in one motion with the same hand. The only time that you'll get fouled up is if somebody's put money in loose. This they aren't supposed to do.

When you open the cover, down goes the loose money into the snow. If you've got the wind just right, it can suck the mail right out of the box. I've had this happen once. A woman was at the window and watched me drive up and open the mailbox, and saw her envelope with money go flying across the field and out through the orchard, and that was the end of that.

A lot of people are getting so they don't want packages left, whether it's because so many of them are working, or they're afraid somebody is going to take it. I keep a list right here in front of me of people that don't want packages left. If you make a mistake and leave one, you're liable for it.

I've never been bitten, but I usually try to play it a little bit cautious until I know a dog. A package had set in the post office for three or four days, and the person put a note out, "Will you bring this to the house and set it just inside the door?" Gee, the German shepherd was standing on the other side of the door, growling quite loudly, so I guessed I wouldn't open the door, I'd leave it right at the door. You have to be careful and not ask for trouble.

Along about the first of October, volume really begins to pick up, getting ready for the Christmas rush. Right after Christmas, income tax refunds come, and the mailers of junk mail really put an effort on for your dollar. During the summer it slacks off and won't pick up again until we get the back-to-school sales.

Some days are busy enough that you don't notice much of anything. But when the mail's fairly light, especially in the summertime, I'm always looking for something different. I'm a bird watcher, and I usually carry my glasses with me. Maybe this is one of the compensations of being on a mail route.

The main disadvantage to the rural-carrier's job is the fact that you have to reach so. Bursitis is called a rural-carrier's disease. Most of us are bothered through our shoulders, arms and back. I don't know as I call working six days a week a disadvantage. I don't want a week where I would be inactive for two days.

I'm on my eleventh year now. There's been a lot of changes. We don't get the mud on the roads we used to. We've got people living on these farms that are not actively engaged in agriculture. The biggest difference is we get more people moving around. Most post offices don't forward the amount of mail that we do. I had a piece of mail that came to "Jane and Sue." I figured out where it went.

You learn things about people by the type of mail they get. Maybe too much so. Maybe sometimes you form opinions. You'll see this type mail coming through and you'll think, "Well, this person is such-and-such a type," and maybe this isn't really so, good or bad.

The most interesting thing on the mail route is people. This is the one thing that keeps it from being monotonous. You have days when you're busy — and real busy — when you like to drive up to the mailbox and get away to make up time. But, by the same token, there are days during the winter when you drive all the way around and don't see anybody. You like to see a face, maybe, just to know that there's life around.

ONE OF THE EARLIEST SIGNS OF SPRING *is the sight of sap buckets hanging along the roadside in Walter Smith's sugarbush. Soon the traveler may roll down the car window to catch a whiff of boiling sap steaming out of the dilapidated sugarhouse. Every March, Paul Brown, a brother-in-law of Kitty Brown, boils sap in Walter's sugarhouse.*

## Paul Brown, 59

I was taught sugarin' 'fore I was ten, probably. We sta'ted in early back then. Everybody had to work. Scatterin' buckets was 'bout the first thing I ever done. Once, I tipped over a load of sap; the sled slid down sideways and throwed the tank off. My father talked to me some, if I remember right.

Got a little older, helped tap, and, when nobody liked to go out, I got to boilin'. Now I don't do much, only boil. Oh, I've been at it about fifty years. I don't know but that's long enough.

Boilin' is just the same as it used to be. Some places they have gas rigs, oil rigs, but we still do it just the way I started, just the way we're doin' it now. The first rig my father had evaporated same as this. Way, way back they used to boil in iron kettles, but that was before my time.

We've had this rig since 1963. We've got to fire it up about every fifteen minutes, generally. I'd say we burn up to fifteen cord. The State has to get rid of old guard rails that's been broken off, so they bring them up here. We have a lot of old rubbish around the farm, usually softwood boards.

We've got some plastic pipeline and probably close to 1300 buckets. We have two rigs picking up. We use a tractor, too. When the sap runs fast, we have to boil nights, see. *Then* you're really busy. I don't stay all night; I stay t'about midnight and come back about four. You don't get much sleep for two or three nights.

The sap boils away faster at night than it does in the daytime. There's something about the night air. The steam goes up better. That's why I like to start four o'clock in the morning: I can boil more, say, in three hours than I can in four in the middle of the day.

Today is not a good boilin' day: too much wind. It blows across the pans, and the sap won't boil up the way it should. When it's still, that steam goes right straight up. Then you can boil, probably, a third faster than when it's windy.

I keep it from boiling up by dipping a little salt pork on a stick into the sap. You can use milk or butter or oleo. The fat breaks the bubbles down. We probably take off about three gallons an hour when it's really going in good shape. We put it into barrels and can it down to the house.

A lot of people use hydrometers, but I learned with a scoop. When the sap drips off that scoop, it's done. This here will probably be Grade "A," and later in the season you'll get probably all Grade "B" or "C." I like the darker stuff myself. It's got more maple flavor.

Last part of sugarin', the syrup's no good. You sell that to the candy factory. Years ago, most everybody used to sugar-off and put it in five- and ten-pound pails. They sold more sugar than they did syrup, used to. At home we always kept enough for cooking for a whole year.

Most every farmer used to sugar years ago. Now it's gettin' to be a thing of the past. No, nobody seems to care for it. It's monotonous. You have to stay right here. My dog stays with me. Well, I've got to put in a little more fire! I guess.

ROBERT HOURIET LIVES *with several adults and children in the commune, Pie in the Sky, in Beaver Meadow. The enormous house and larger barn, perched on top of a long driveway, are part of the former Earl Dwinell place. A nearby one-room schoolhouse and cemetery bear the same name. Because the commune was renting, Robert didn't feel really settled: "I have an instinct to find a place: to find a sense of place. It's a major reason why people come to Vermont. Towns are still strong. Sense of place is still extant here."*

## Robert Houriet, 37

This is Earl Dwinell's sugarhouse. When we came here, I found all the parts to the rig just where he left them. This is his arch, and this is his pan, and some of his old piping coming up from the leaky holding tank. I was rummaging around for a board to cut up for a brace, and I found one up here in the rafters. I pulled it out, and there was his name right on it. It was very symbolic to pull the man's name out because everything else bore his personality. So instead of using it for just a common brace, I put it across the top of the holding tank, like you put a name on a ship. It's now christened the Earl Dwinell Holding Tank.

I never met Earl, but sometimes I come back late at night and feel like he's hanging around here. I have certain poetic fantasies about old, deceased sugarmakers who once tapped the same trees. Some of these large maple trees are over two hundred years old. You find these little tap holes in them — they look like a closed eyelid squinting at you — and you realize they were made by someone over a hundred years ago.

I'm not always out here alone. Other people come around and help out. We drink beer and eat pickles and boil knockwurst and potatoes in the syrup pan and listen to WQXR. Earl probably had a drink now and then. I know he did. I found a lot of bottles around. His wife wouldn't let him drink in the house. He used to go out behind the barn. That's the story, anyway.

Earl Dwinell was not my father or even my relative, but it's important to have a sense of continuity — that you are part of an ongoing process. I want to know where I came from. It's something which people around here know. It's handed down: oral history. But in the kind of society I came from, somehow all that history's roots were forgotten.

I grew up in the industrial town of Akron, Ohio. My father was a time-study efficiency expert in a factory, designing ways to make tires go faster. He didn't like automobiles. He realized the absurdity of what he was doing. He would have much preferred the simpler life: fishing and hunting. He didn't have a context in which to question that system, so he worked thirty-five years and had a heart attack.

I've got to fire this now. See how the coals have got low? It's not the best wood. The way the old-timers did it — the way Earl did it, I suppose — was to cut the wood the summer before and let it dry really well. Then you've got good sugar wood. Not like us hippies do and cut it as we use it. Being in one place, you get a rhythm of knowing you cut your wood at a certain time. Always moving around, you can't.

You talk about self-sufficiency. Is it better to be doing this rather than working for a corporation? I'd rather put my energy into working on what I want to do rather than working for someone else in a dehumanizing way. It gets back to the American corporate structure: nine-to-five jobs that don't mean very much to the people who manufacture the products or who sell them or buy them.

I was on the boundaries of the nine-to-five corporate structure in that I was working for newspapers. I was night editor for a paper outside of Philadelphia. My ambition was to be a managing editor. But a number of things happened: we didn't have editorial latitude to do stories about the black-nationalist movement; I couldn't keep reporters because the pay was inadequate. The final straw was my best reporter had hair down to his shirt collar. I could not continue to be editor if I was going to have to fire him because he hadn't cut his hair. So I quit. That was about the time of the 1968 Democratic Convention in Chicago.

Excuse me, what's happening here is that the syrup pan is filling full of small bubbles and foam which are indicative of the approaching syrup. You can test it with a hydrometer for specific gravity and tell if it's syrup. The old-timers didn't use that. All they did was eyeball it. If the first drops off a scoop form an apron, not a drip, they call it syrup. This was Earl's scoop. I put a new handle on it.

So I went to the Democratic Convention, not as a reporter but as a participant. I got tear-gassed and chased by the police. It was an experience that changed me in some ways. I began seriously thinking about social change and what it meant to be, not a revolutionary — yeah, I guess, a revolutionary.

I'm going to test again. It's 31 points on the hydrometer, so it's got two points to go for syrup. It's cooking well.

On the way back from Chicago I stopped at a commune in Pennsylvania that was being harassed by the police. I interviewed them and wrote a story for *The New York Times Magazine* about a commune and its relationship with straight society.

On the basis of that magazine article, I got offers from six publishers to do a book. So I went around the country and visited communes and wrote a book about it. It was still a professional assignment. I was out to make a buck off of the counterculture. I was sympathetic, but not involved.

Whoops! I just put some evaporated milk in the syrup to make the

foam go down. It boiled faster than I thought it would. It still reads 31. It looks like syrup, though.

I did some acid and went though a lot of spiritual trips and got very excited about the whole concept of living communally. In the last chapter of the book I mentioned I was interested in living that way, and, if anyone else was, we should go in together. And, lo and behold, people actually were foolish enough to take up the offer. Four couples got together and bought a farm in Vermont.

I left there because my relationship with my wife broke up. We had taken on too much too fast. I began doing food co-op work. I wanted to have background material to write a book. I got swallowed up in the work and haven't written the book. I'm trained as a writer, but I'd rather farm right now.

The basis of our society has been agriculture. The way this society has developed has been to exploit its agriculture and to mechanize it and to ruin it, to develop a system which puts farmers out of work and puts machines in their places: agribusiness. I personally want to work for a lifetime and see a new farming system developed as the basis of a new society.

This is particularly American in the Jeffersonian tradition of a decentralized society. A number of people came to this country to be free of centralized controls, political or religious or military. But once the frontier closed, those same centralized controls began to reimpose themselves. The newest form is corporate controls.

In this generation the typical American response to those controls is to go back to the land. We're all part of the same movement—to go back. Some people are going back further than others, but we're all moving in the same direction. I don't want to go back all the way. God! I'd hate to think of cutting all this sugaring wood with a two-man saw.

That's pretty damn close to syrup. By the time I get around to going through my gyrations, it will be syrup. I'm drawing off. Here it comes. We've got a good gallon there.

As one of the true "bridge" people *in the community, Lucille Cerutti is firmly planted in the traditional rural society, but has worked for years at Goddard College—first in the kitchen, then in the housing office, and in psychological services. She relishes gossip—"None of it's been really vicious gossip today"—and, predictably, hears her share.*

## Lucille Cerutti, 49

Spring's really a nice time of year. It's fun to watch the woods come alive. The trees take on a pink hue. When the buds begin to come, the hillsides are beautiful shades of green. The evergreens begin to glimmer and shine. They're all sparkly, like trees after a storm. Just after the snow is gone, I go out and get pussy willows. The ground cover will begin to perk up soon. You can go out and pick fiddlehead ferns and cowslips and dandelions. Then you watch for the violets.

You watch for the killdeer and the red-winged blackbirds and the meadowlarks first. The robins come soon after. You're really excited the morning the tree swallows come back. Soon we'll begin to see the warblers and the ruby-crowned kinglets. I know only one person that's seen a bluebird this year.

I really don't enjoy the mud. It always comes, sometimes worse than others, depending on what the winter was like and how the ditches thawed out to drain the road off. They don't make cars today to go wanderin' around in muddy roads. When you had cars that were way up off the ground, you could go right through a mud hole. If you couldn't, why, you stopped and threw some stones in under the wheels and run along.

I don't think you're going to be able to afford to hop in your car and go for a leisure ride. Gas costs a lot of money—60 cents a gallon. Maybe it'll go up some more. I think people have been a little bitter, don't you? And have not consented to the fact that they can't come and go like they have. I don't see any signs of the people mingling more together. That's why I think they're setting back, feeling a little resentful, and haven't figured out their mode of entertainment.

For a long, long time it was just country people here, people who'd been here all their lives. We used to dance and play cards and get together, just because. Gossip was always a part of people's lives. You knew more what people were thinking and doing. Our lives were more intertwined.

We had an encounter group in our office at Goddard. Maybe some people can improve their hang-ups by talking with other people, but I don't think that would come easy to a Vermonter. You'd do better to go up in the woods and have a talk with yourself.

Of all the people in our office I'm the only dyed-in-the-wool Vermonter. They said that a lot of times they just didn't understand what I meant. That meeting made me set back on my heels and do a lot of thinking. I said right out loud, "Right now, I'm as close to being a red-necked Vermonter as I've ever been in all my life." I didn't like any part of that feeling. It brought to my mind very clearly that we just didn't understand each other very well.

If you reversed the situation—if you moved all the country people to the city—would those city people protect their territory? This is our territory. You've come to our territory. If they're going to live here, they're going to have to understand it's not easy to go through a Vermont winter. Living in Vermont is not easy.

City people are unaware of the people around them. I was waiting for someone from my office. I stood right out in the road near a big elm tree at Goddard. She drove right by me, turned around, came back and parked, and never saw me till she walked back up. When I teased her about it, she said she was lookin' for a place to park. There's no way I could drive up and down that road twice and not see a whole lot of things *while* I was looking for a parking place. Maybe it's just because my scope is wider.

TO GET AN ACTIVE SEVEN-YEAR-OLD TO TALK *with you for fifteen minutes, even about the long-awaited marble season, is a wonder. Yet Matthew—the youngest child of Norman and Sallie Dix, who operate one of the two trash businesses in the area—demonstrated complicated marble strategies for me on a little oval rug in his bedroom. As soon as I thanked him for the interview, he shot out the door to play ball with Bill and Corinne Smith's kids next door.*

## Matthew Dix, 8

LINDA: Are there special names for the kinds of marbles you have?

MATTHEW: Yeah. I've got one Chinese jumbo and one alley. I've got one half-Chinese and a Chinese alley. It's as big as an alley, but it's Chinese. And I got one bumblebee—with the little black wings on it you call it a bumblebee—and I got one solid alley. The black alleys are the best. And I got a pure. You can see through it. I would say the Chinese jumbo is worth the most.

LINDA: Who decides which marbles are worth what?

MATTHEW: There are rules you have to follow

LINDA: Do you mostly play with kids your own age?

MATTHEW: I play some kids in the third grade and some fourth graders and some second graders. I don't play with a kid in the second grade 'cause he cheats. If the duty teacher comes and talks to you, and you're looking that way, he puts his marble in, saying he won the game.

LINDA: Do you play mostly boys or girls?

MATTHEW: Mostly boys.

LINDA: Do the girls play mostly with themselves?

MATTHEW: Uh-huh.

LINDA: Do you think the boys are better at marbles than the girls?

MATTHEW: No, I don't think so. The girls are pretty good at it, too.

LINDA: Are you a pretty good marble player?

MATTHEW: Uh-huh.

LINDA: What kind of marble games do you play?

MATTHEW: Long ones.

LINDA: Say you and I were going to play marbles now. What would you say?

MATTHEW: "Boots and fings; no buttercups."

LINDA: What does "boots" mean?

MATTHEW: You shoot a marble over to the pot with your hand and call "boots." You take your foot, and you hit your other foot that the marble's by, and the marble goes rolling away towards the pot.

LINDA: Can you tell me what "fings" means?

MATTHEW: You take your second knuckle on your finger and throw the marble toward the pot.

LINDA: And what was "no buttercups"?

MATTHEW: If you shoot the marble hard enough, it'll go right through the pot. If you shoot it hard with buttercups, it'll bounce off your two feet and roll into the pot.

LINDA: Are there any other variations?

MATTHEW: You have picksies. Your marble goes right in the pot, and his marble goes about a centimeter away. You pick it up and throw it to the pot, and if it rolls in, you win. Then there's backsies. If you don't dare to shoot to the pot, you fing it backward so the other guy can't get it in. And there's sidesies—same as backsies, but it's sidesies.

LINDA: When does marble season begin?

MATTHEW: You play from the first day of spring, when the snow and mud get away, to the last day of school. You can play all summer if you want, but the ground is hard then.

LINDA: Why does the ground have to be soft?

MATTHEW: So you can make the pot. You stick your heel in loose dirt and turn around and around and hollow it out.

LINDA: How old are the kids when they start playing marbles?

MATTHEW: About five. In kindergarten.

LINDA: And how old are they when they stop?

MATTHEW: In the sixth grade. They don't have recess.

LINDA: What will you do with your collection when you're too old to play?

MATTHEW: Keep it for when I grow up or maybe trade it for some money. I traded an alley for twelve cents.

LINDA: What did you do with the twelve cents?

MATTHEW: Spent it.

LINDA: On candy?

MATTHEW: No, on more marbles.

WHERE LUCILLE CERUTTI AND MATTHEW DIX *live almost across the road from each other at the bottom of the hill, Kitty Brown lives among kin in houses clustered together on "the Brown road." In Kitty's small house, spring means attempting to hatch some eggs. Although she obviously cares for both eggs and chicks, the operation is largely a challenge, an education, a joke, while failure is met with a laugh—if there's a good story in it.*

## Kitty Brown, 44

I don't know if you'd call it foolish or a good move, but my sister, Betty, and I decided we was going to have some chickens. My husband says, "I'm not going to fool with them," and I said, "You don't have to, I will." He says, "It'll be just the same as your other projects," he says, "you won't tend to them." And I said, "Don't you worry about it." The eggs from my dear old pullets clear me about $6 a week over the feed.

We've had a lot of fun in this hatching business. I gathered thirty eggs from my own flock and turned them faithfully in a small incubator. I'd keep looking if there wa'n't one least crack in them. Nawthin. People would call me, "Got any chicks yet, Kitty?" and I'd say, "No."

The first of May at quarter past five the alarm went off. My husband fixed his coffee and got back in bed and said, "Say, Mawr," he says, "you've got a chick coming out." I says, "I have not." So he says, "I'm not fooling, you get up and see." I said, "April Fool's Day is gone." He kept at me, so I decided I'd get up. And, sure enough, here was this tiny hole in that egg.

I was so tickled. It kept shrugging its shoulders. I don't know what you call them—shoulders, maybe, on a chicken? I called my daughter up and said, "Do you want to come down here when they're hatching?" 'cause she called every forenoon: "Got any chicks yet?" Well, by the time I got off the telephone, that chicken had jumped out of its shell.

We babied this poor chick along, and it seemed to get livelier on the second day. When I came home that night, he was a-making a lot of noise. "What's the matter with you? Didn't you spend a good afternoon?" I was talking away to it and decided to pick it up. Well, that was a wrong move. That chicken jumped out and landed on the floor. It killed him. I've always told the kids, "Be careful, don't handle them," and here I am forty-four years old, and it was gone.

We've talked to everybody about hatching these chicks to see if we couldn't find some answers. My sister was talking with Dr. Merrill when she had to take her boy into the emergency room. He said, "Well, how are you?" 'Course, she always brings up subjects; she brought up the subject of turning eggs. He said that when he turned his six times a day instead of three, he got better livability.

My sister was talking with a fellow up in Cabot. "I'll tell you," he says, "you must be doing something wrong." And she says, "We know that, but we don't know what." "Well," he says, "the best thing is an electric frying pan." And my sister said, "What?"

He says, "I wouldn't have believed it if I hadn't seen it," but he said the next-door neighbor's hen started setting on eggs and for some reason wouldn't finish them. So the woman scooped up the eggs and put them in her electric frying pan and turned it way down low, and the chicks hatched. I may have to try that to get chicks.

I had three roosters running with my thirty-two pullets. I don't know if I ever told you, "Watch out for the black rooster 'cause he's ugly." Oh, he used to pick at me. I was scared to go out and collect my eggs. My grandchildren couldn't go outdoors to play. He never touched my husband. My husband would say, "See? He's just as calm as a cucumber."

One day I told that ugly rooster, "Just one more time, and you're going to lose your head." For two days he'd tried to get me. He was in the chicken-house door. I said, "You stay right in there, mister; don't you chase me." He didn't come out the door. I thought I had him conquered. I decided to look back, and he was flying right at my face.

My husband came home and I said, "He's got to go." So we chopped his head off and I said to my daughter, "Do you want to take him home?" He must have dressed out six or eight pounds. She put him in a pan and just half of him fed five. My father came along and said, "Where did you get that?" She said, "Gramp, that Mawr's ugly rooster." My father says, "He'll probably fly right out of that pan and pick you when you go to eat him!"

CECIL METCALF, JR., TRASH MAN, *is in love with his work. He loves the physical challenges—swinging onto the back gate of his 1972 Chevy truck, swinging a container over the side, then swinging down to the ground while pulling his work gloves on tighter. But he also loves the mental challenges— testing for valuable metals, guessing if the results of every housewife's spring cleaning will appear the same week, observing the landscape: "Isn't that a view?"*

## Cecil Metcalf, Jr., 33

I had only twenty-five customers when I started the trash route eight years ago. Now I have three hundred stops a week. It keeps me out of mischief four and a half days a week. I'm buildin' a house the rest of the time.

For four years I did this durin' the day and worked nights down to the State Capitol doin' janitor work. I worked the graveyard shift, 11:00 to 7:00. I'd get the work all done in four hours, then take a nap. I got in a mess tryin' to work around the clock like that. The only thing that was keepin' me awake was whiskey.

I'm not a heavy drinker now. To be honest with you, I have a limit and stick right with it pretty good. I drink just a six-pack a day. I drink a couple while I'm around on the route, usually, and, while I'm up at the new house, it just makes my work go along a little easier to have a beer sittin' there. My wife, she don't care.

I don't really like to be under pressure. I like to stay casual, stay easy. You've got to admit it's an easy atmosphere. If the people like you, and you do a good job to satisfy them, you got it made because the rest falls into place naturally. From ridin' around, you learn where the good sources of information are. Everybody around here has a trade, or they're handy in one way or another. I feel I know everybody real close on the trash route. I'm so content, it's unbelievable.

A guy works for me Monday, Wednesday and Friday. He usually just helps lug the cans out. I never let him jump up on the back of the truck. I don't get him in a position where he's goin' to get hurt 'cause that costs money. I don't carry any of that workmen's compensation insurance on him, so I just look out for him. He's fifty-eight years old, but his mentality, they claim, is somewhere between twelve and fourteen.

The truck's insured, heavily. You treat that truck with the fullest respect, and it will last forever. I've been runnin' this route on this day for six years. Might have had to stop and fix the truck in the middle of the day, but we always made it sometime between now and midnight.

The worst part is the bookkeeping. You've got to keep track of all your expenses. I never put any pressure on anybody, and I don't ever lose my money, either. Some pay each week. Some pay six times a year. There's a lot of weeks I don't make very big, and there's weeks I make damn good. My take-home pay is about $10,000 a year.

There's got to be a lot of money in trash because the guy that owns the dump buys $120,000 worth of bulldozers to bury it with. He drives a Cadillac to work. He owns a big beautiful home. He seems to have no problems, and all he's doin' is wallowin' around that stuff all day.

Everybody has a little different system of puttin' trash up. One house has two trash cans. The next house has one plastic bag. They always have them two barrels and a little ga'bage pail. Week after week you know exactly what you're goin' to find. It's consistent. Every single Thursday I put 500 cubic feet of trash from forty houses in that truck. There's a never-endin' supply of it.

You get your seasonal trash, but it balances out throughout the year. You get rakings in the spring and fall. Some people compost them, but the majority throw them away. I have a busy summer, but I make good money. I got a hundred stops more in the summer between July first and Labor Day. That's how many people don't live here year-round. At Christmas time you get Christmas trees and wrappings. Spring and fall you get house and attic cleanin'.

Today there was a green plastic trash bag half-full of doughnuts and cookies. I didn't want to sort it out after I had dumped it, but, if I'd noticed it quicker, I'd have waited till I got up beside of the road somewhere and dumped it for the birds. I pick up suet at a store and jump out and leave it in the crotch of an elm tree. I had chickadees all winter long. I get bones out of the store's rubbish and keep them in my chain box for different dogs around the route. Still, I have dog problems like any travelin' peddler.

People around here have an awful lot of pets: guinea hens, geese, banty hens. They're tryin' to get back to the old-time ways. Those type people don't make any trash. They're livin' off the land. They're self-sufficient, really. Wood is their only source of fuel; they raise their garden like you wouldn't believe.

It's just like us when we had our farm years ago. We went to the dump maybe twice a year. We had to go shoppin' to the city maybe once a month for supplies. We had to go after cornmeal for cornmeal bread, 'cause we ate a lot of that, and flour. Our butter and cottage cheese was sent over from the creamery. My mother canned between five and six hundred quarts a year, besides jellies and jams and pickles.

The bank put my father up there for $2,100 — 160 acres, house and barn, cattle, a team of horses, what farm machinery he needed to get started — and when he sold it fifteen years later, he still owed $2,100. He just paid the interest. The bank never cared. They liked him, I guess.

It's a get-rich-quick world today. There's probably not enough jobs in the area that pay that good to hold people. Local young kids don't seem to be lookin' for to build or buy to keep the area local. This is prominent on people's minds. You can see it is on mine.

It's people that didn't know a free life that are comin' to this area where the houses are thinned out. In the cities somebody's only got a hundred-foot-square piece of land. That's the extent of their freedom. People feel they can't even step out their front door after the first sign of dark comes. Your house is the only place you're safe, and then you're not. It looks like a hellhole to me. How many places can you live in the world where you can walk out a mile and really feel safe? You can here.

I used to carry my rod right in the truck and stop halfway around the route and fish. I wasn't married then; I didn't have anybody to hurry home to. I've got the same fish pole now for ten years. It cost a whole sum, when I bought that reel, of a dollar and ninety-nine cents. I never use any artificial lures for brook trout. All I use for bait is worms. Just worms, right out of the manure pile.

I can tell you the whole secret of fishin'. You just don't walk down the brook and catch a meal of fish. It takes patience and time. You just gotta set there and wait for the fish to make up his mind. It's relaxin'. You'd be tired, you'd be dirty, you'd be all mixed up in your mind — and the best way to clear your mind is to grab that fish pole and head right for the brook.

# Summer

BETWEEN MEMORIAL DAY AND LABOR DAY occurs that shortest of seasons, the longest hoped for: summer. To avoid a late, killing frost, gardens are planted the last weekend in May. Our soil, referred to as "dark Cabot loam," is ideal for corn, if only the early September frosts hold off. By summer solstice we say, shamelessly, "We deserve this," knowing that as of this day the enlarged light will start to dim.

Fourth of July parades initiate true summer. With eyes squinting against the unaccustomed light, we witness our neighbors' lightly clothed forms. An active visibility pervades the landscape: leaf light shimmering in the woods; restless, nesting birds; heifers fattening on the wide grass; germinating beans; fireflies in the dark fields. Each day is perfect, and we start to trust that this brief sweetness may endure long enough for us to complete the summer's labor.

Throughout the abundant days of July, the green of woods and fields multiplies under a generous sky. Windrows in cut fields look like green corduroy. In a day or two, the baler will pack the hay into tight rectangles. Contrariwise, another farmer rolls his hay into "cinnamon buns." Entire families shepherd tractors, pulling loaded hay wagons, from field to barn.

The lowering heat of August brings out the fleas on domestic animals, then ripens the blackberries, tomatoes and Queen Anne's lace. Pumpkins start to yellow around the stem. Trees' shadows change from a dark green to grey. By Bennington Battle Day, in the middle of the month, there is a sense of hurrying to finish the last weeding, wood-stacking, painting, fixing-up.

That two friends should be walking up the hill on a dark night, in the fullness of August, and talk about their dread of winter — this must be said. But one has already picked up a first fallen red leaf on the road. Thistledown drifts across the cooling fields. In the morning a white mist conceals marshes and ponds. Blackbirds and grackles have begun to flock. The lower branches of roadside trees are heavy with dust. School begins in a week. We anticipate the first frost.

THERE IS NOTHING ABSTRACT *about a vegetable garden. There is planning before planting, of course, but, as Bea Robertson says, "I'm sort of experimenting." That leads to mixing radish seeds in with the lettuce, giving one more reason to "go to the garden" the first week in June.*

## Bea Robertson, 59

It always seemed like home up here on this hill. I lived in Hardwick for a while, but I really don't care for village living. I like the location here. I'm not a green thumb, but I seem to have more interest now than I used to about gardening. This soil here is quite rich, but it would do it good to have some lime to sweeten it. This is new ground so I thought I'd have a pretty good crop of weeds this year.

I started in with potatoes and peas soon as I got the garden roto-vated somewhere between the seventh and the tenth of June. I bought potatoes for eating, but they seemed to be getting by me, so I thought, well, I'd put them in the ground and see if they'd grow. I left two eyes on each piece. That's the way the folks at home taught me to cut pota-toes for planting. You hill them up so it makes a big fat bed for the potatoes to lay their eggs in. When the leaves die on the plant, you dig them. These potatoes here are some of those first ones I planted. Five fill three-quarters of my hand.

I put in my tomatoes and corn and carrots, and beets for beet greens, and cucumbers, pumpkins, squash. I planted it a day or two at a time if the mosquitoes didn't bite too bad. I wish we had some chickens to

eat up the grasshoppers 'cause we have a good crop right now. I see them jumpin' in front of me when I go to the garden.

As fast as the peas would blossom, the deer come along and clean them right down. Then they got into my beans. I decided, well, I've got to do something or I'm going to lose everything. I put up a scarecrow. I used one of these towel trees that you hang towels on, and stuffed some paper bags inside a shirt, and somebody's old trousers and hat.

Then my son borrowed a dog and hitched him right beside of the garden. It seems to keep the deer at a certain distance. I don't think the woodchucks have bothered. There was a little path, and I didn't know but there might be a muskrat. A variety of animals have passed through this section. We've seen deer and a fisher cat over the years. I used to feed hens, so we used to see quite a lot of foxes. My husband hates animals. He hates everything of that sort that lives and breathes.

My hobby was raising animals. We've had pigs and calves and sheep and horses and dogs and cats and rabbits and chickens. The only colt I ever raised was born the 30th day of March, cutest little thing standing up aside of the fence. Oh, she was so dear I could've put her in my pocket. I had to give her away when she was three years old.

Walter Smith gave me a little lamb when it was just a few days old. I brought it up on the bottle. He used to lay out on the step and eye people when they'd come in. I don't think some of them dared to go by him. My husband was one of them. He and the sheep didn't get along, so the sheep had to go in the fall.

HELEN MACDONALD'S ORIGINS *are in a Greek family from Washington, D.C. She lives with her husband, Bruce, an employee of the Vermont State Department of Budget and Management, and their two young daughters in the only single-family housing development on the hill. In addition to goats, they manage to raise "donkeys, lambs, calves, chickens, ducks, geese, a little heifer. We do very well with this little patch of ground."*

## Helen MacDonald, 36

My husband had a goat when he was a youngster, and he swore for years he'd get one for our kids. He called me one day from work — no preparation, no nothing — and said he was bringing a goat home. I didn't want it. To make a long story short, we got one, it had a baby, and the next thing you know we've got all these goats.

The first thing I thought was, "My God, he can't put it in the garage." I found out later, and it's important that people know, that they do not smell if you keep them clean. They're economical. They do not eat tin cans. If they drop their hay, they will not eat it if it hits the floor.

Raising goats made an unbelievable difference to me, personally. I used to get very bored. I'm a very active person. If I don't move all the time, I get nervous. I get up at 5:30, usually manage to throw a cup of coffee down, and run out of the house by twenty minutes to six. We feed the goats while we milk because they're not apt to put their foot in the bucket. They know what order they go in and jump up on their own milk stand. They lounge around until you're ready to hay them. We clean the barn once a week all the way through, and during the week I throw down added bedding.

At the beginning my husband did all the milking. Well, he got sick and couldn't milk, and, ohhh, I was terrorized, but he had 104 temperature. I had no idea how to milk except I used to watch him. I was really scared because goats are smart. If you're afraid of them, they'll kick their heels up or put their foot in the bucket or simply leave. You look around, and your goat's gone. If you're very firm, they'll calm right down and behave.

Well, this goat took off and I put her back on the stand, and she took off again and I spanked her. I got one cup from her that night—one cup! That was all. I had it in a jar and ran upstairs and showed my husband. I said, "Look! I told you I could do it!" I was really proud of myself. After that I started milking every other morning. He never milks unless I'm very ill.

Goat people are akin to fishermen: they tell you these stories. Not true! If you get half a gallon of milk per day, you've got a good goat. If you get a gallon out of her, she's doing great. I almost sold my big goat because everyone kept telling me, "She's not giving but three cups." That was her first time to kid. Now she's up where she should be.

After our first one kidded, I put off drinking her milk. I wouldn't touch it. I'd look at it and think, "Eventually, I'm going to have to taste that." Well, one day Sallie Dix came up, and I say, "Okay, Sallie, today's the day we're going to taste this." When I think back, I have hysterics. She said, "You go first," and I said, "No, you go first." I finally put a teaspoon in and took the first taste. I was shocked. I couldn't believe how good it was. I had heard that goats' milk was terrible. Phooey!

It's all in how you raise your goats. Usually, the fate of a goat is to live on a farm with eighty cows and no special place for that goat. She's forced to sleep where she might have to lay down in manure. Her milk will become off-flavored if the barn smells.

I always have my own milk supply. It's fun to be able to run out and say, "C'mon, Dais'," if I feel like making a pudding. I love when the milkman comes every year with this big grin on his face and says to me, "I know you won't," he says, "but I'm supposed to go to every door. Do you want to take milk?" It makes me feel very good to say, "No, thank you."

Right now we have six goats. I have five females, and a buck which we use for stud service. You bring the doe in and let the buck loose, and nature takes it course. It depends on the stage of the heat, but quite often the buck will service her immediately. After this, there's quite a nice little ritual they do. He'll make this fantastic noise in her ears. It's quite a cute thing.

It would appear to us that their sexual life is in extreme reverse of ours. They get on with it! — they have the intercourse part — and then the courtship comes after. It's hilarious, but that's how they do it, and they're perfectly happy. Five minutes later you collect $8, and that's it.

The normal gestation for most goats is 150 to 155 days. Most always, there's no assistance needed. They can have from one single birth to quadruplets. You keep the goat if you want a herd replacement, or you can sell her for $30, $35. Some people sell them for meat, which I find difficult. You get attached. We kept one back for meat, and, fates will have it, he ended up being the nicest one.

Mine are so spoiled that they're apt to beller if they're hungry and don't have enough hay, which presents some problems with your neighbors. People will call you and say, "Hey, did you know your little goat is out there with her head stuck in a bucket?" So, no matter what you're doing, you have to drop it and go run out to the barn. But I love that. I'd just as soon drop it. That's my way out.

RICHARD HUTCHINSON, CALLED "DICKIE," *is one of the fairly steady farm hands seen over the years, walking the cows up to pasture or dumping milk in the cooler or mending fence or crossing the road from the barn to the house at Walter Smith's farm. Dickie was raised on a farm. "In this area?" I asked. "No, around Barre, Graniteville, Williamstown and East Montpelier, mostly, but not too much up this way," said he, familiar with the diversity of farm work attempted on different kinds of days.*

## Richard Hutchinson, 42

This is what you call a variety farm — you're always chasin' somethin'. I've worked here, oh, eight, nine years, off and on. I worked for two years steady, then wasn't satisfied with the wages, so I went out paintin'. The fellow I was paintin' with, he died, so I come back to farmin'. I'm just fillin' in part-time until Walt gets another hired man. I help milk the cows and get the cows and mow and rake and put in the hay.

When I first got this job, he said to me, he said, "Could you milk cows?" And I says, "I'll tell you, Walt, I don't quite understand these milkin' machines, but," I says, "it won't take me but a few minutes to figure 'em out 'cause I can run any kind of machine." He says, "Well, that's good," said, "we had another kid there, and he wasn't gettin' up in the mornin', wasn't makin' the milk." I ran the machines, and cows come up on milk. Last night I milked 'em all alone.

We're milkin' fifty-four now, but there's sixty in all, supposed to be. We got some goin' dry. It takes about an hour and a half to milk 'em with four machines. They figure about three minutes to a cow. I have to run back and forth, check each quarter to see if it's all milked out perfectly. If it don't, you get in bag trouble.

It's bad to overmilk 'em. It injures the muscles where the milk flows out through. Then they either go on three-titter, or she'll come down with acute mastitis. That acute mastitis will kill a cow within twelve hours. It's about four or five different kinds of mastitis that you have to watch for every single time.

Every cow is different. Some are nervous when you milk 'em. They'll like to twitch a little bit, not what you'd call kick. They like to tread a little bit, too, and switch their tails. They don't have to be no flies on 'em. You may not have any trouble with a nice quiet one, and within three, four days she may kick. It all depends how they feel. Some days they feel crankier, just like a person.

The worst problem we have is gettin' the cows up and down from the pasture. We can start after the cows at 3:00, 3:30 in the afternoon, and sometimes we won't get out until 5:30. If the cows are not too hot with no flies botherin' 'em, they all hang together, but as soon as the flies start chasin' 'em, you have to comb that woods all out. They've got about 300 acres to roam into, with more woods'n there is open.

I get behind 'em and holler, "Go on, cows," or something like that. "Get movin'!" Sometimes you can holler your head off, and they won't move. When they get too much punishment, the cows will figure, "Well, what's the use of us comin'? You come after us."

A little while back, three of 'em was missin', but we met 'em comin' down the roadway. We figured, "Well, golly, they'll stay until we get the rest," see, "then we'll let the fence down and let 'em run right on home." But when we went to get the other ones, lo and behold, those three were gone: number 8, 51 and 21. Uhyuh. We didn't care about two of 'em because they were goin' dry anyways, but that 21 hadn't been milked for three days.

Now, I come home for dinner about one o'clock, I said to Walt, I said, "I betcha a dollar to doughnuts they're in with the heifers." Well,

Walt said they couldn't be; the fence was fixed good, couldn't be. So, golly sakes, somebody called up five o'clock in the mornin', said that those three cows are over in the heifers' patch. That 21 cow filled that milkin' machine up twice.

I can tell you somethin' about a cow. A cow is a lot smarter than what you think they are, but sometimes you get so mad at 'em, you think they're awful stupid. Oh, once in a while I'll have to take the palm of my hand and make 'em straighten out; otherwise it would kick the devil right out of me. I quit a job one time 'cause I don't believe in poundin' cows up. The farmer said, "You hit 'em with your hands, don't yuh?" I said, "Yes, but," I says, "it hurts my hands more'n it does them."

WHERE A HUNDRED YEARS AGO *Thompson's* History of Vermont *could proclaim that "six-sevenths of the whole population are engaged in agricultural pursuits," in our time, farming is the work of the few and the memory of the old. The hand-placed stone walls of two hundred years ago tumble into the underbrush. Barns rot away from their granite foundations. Land is cleared for the view, not for grazing animals or for the fields to feed them. Land-based skills, and the social conventions surrounding them, belong largely to the past. Three remnants of that past speak here. The first, Walter Smith, is described by some who know him.*

> *Walter Smith's farm is the meetinghouse of the world. I really admire him for being able to get things done at all.* — DALE LINDER, A NEIGHBOR.
>
> *I have always had to do with Walter Smith. He's a uniquely open person and a good neighbor. He will speak of a place or person which I happen not to know about. In a very nice way, he includes me. He takes for granted that you are an inhabitant of the same province.* — JULES RABIN

*There cannot be a more country person here than Walter Smith. His mind is wide open, but in lots of ways Walter holds his place. I'm aware that some people don't understand a lot of things that he does. I'm from the same world Walter is, so I understand every word that he says. It sure is fascinating to watch him.* — LUCILLE CERUTTI

*Eat and run! Eat and run! One morning, Walter was going to eat his oatmeal. He looked at the spoon he had, and he looked at the clock and said, 'Oooop, don't have long; I'm going to have to get a bigger spoon.' Eat and run!* — SUSAN DUNN, A GODDARD COLLEGE STUDENT RENTING A ROOM FROM WALTER SMITH.

## Walter Smith, 62

I was brought up on the old family farm in Richford, up on the Canadian line. That farm was about 350 acres. Some farmers raised wheat, and some raised barley. My father always raised oats. My uncle and my father owned a thrashing machine together. We'd go from one farm to another and thrash the grain in the fall and the first part of winter.

My father used to go with a team of horses and a set of double sleds to get his flour and his sugar and his cornmeal—we ate a lot of johnnycake—and salt salmon in kegs and bring it home to the farm. In the first of the winter the meat was put in the meat box. We threw water around it and froze it out back in the snow. When it came spring, that meat had to be taken out and cooked and canned. We all felt pretty bad when my father sold the old farm.

I got out of school right in the Depression. I worked for a dollar a day and my board on another farm where we peddled milk with a horse. Then I went into the creamery to work. I came up to run this farm in '38. When I bought here, there were seventy-three farms in the town of Marshfield alone. Now about six or seven are shipping milk. You mention that to these government men, and, "Well," they say, "those farms are still there." But on those farms those fields grow up to brush, or they're planted to Christmas trees.

It hurts these towns. It's a better economy for the towns to have twenty small farms than one large one. That large one operates much more economical, but those twenty farms—where the people were living off from them, producing their goods and paying taxes—were keeping the land up.

At home we didn't go to the store every day. You lived off the farm. That's one thing I try to do here. The only meat we buy is fish. We have plenty of chickens. We have our eggs, and we have our milk, and I raise my own potatoes, and I put in a garden. It's hard to get those things taken care of now that my wife is dead. She died six years ago last November of emphysema.

After my wife died, the sharpies were here. One said, "Why don't you sell out and go to Florida?" Florida wouldn't interest me a bit. And why should I sell? See, there's 500 acres here now. They'd break that up into ten-acre lots. People have just about worn me out for building lots.

I got a nice lumber lot down in there. Every fellow and his cousin's been after me to log that. Well, I won't let them. I can use that lumber here on the farm. One thing I didn't specify in my will was I wanted it left so no one would ever go through and slash my sugar place. It takes a hundred years for a maple to grow to maturity, and about thirty-five years to where you can tap them.

I've got so many things going it's never-ending. Before we started sugaring, we were getting some logs. I've sold a little hay. I sold some corn. We hayed all last summer right through until corn-harvesting time. I like to fill all those barns right up full. I'll probably raise more wheat this year than I want for myself. I'm going to make a deal with Charlie Carpenter up to Cabot so as he will reap and thrash it for me.

Equipment is a big item on these farms. The old hay wagon was bought 'way back during the war when we couldn't get tires for our cars. My old car was badly in need of them, so I bought the wagon and took the tires off it. You try to make things go a little longer than you should, rather than make a trade. If I trade tractors, you've got to pay a sales tax. On a $12,000 tractor, it's terrific.

We've all gotten so disgusted with the government taking it away from us, more than we'll ever get back if we live to be ninety. It's better for a workingman to have what he earns and use it wisely, than it is to have the government tangle into it.

I'd like to see the state go back to where we were forty years ago and operate within our own means. There are too many men in Montpelier and Washington that think they are smart enough to run everyone's business from back of a desk with their feet up. We don't need those men. It's a waste of our tax dollars.

A dollar is synthetic. It's only worth what you can buy with it. I sometimes wonder if we've got as much gold as we think we have to back it. Your banks are only as secure as your government. We're nearing a depression now. We've got inflation. If this oil situation doesn't ease, we're really going to be hit.

If I thought things were really going bad, one of the first things I'd do is go up into Canada and buy me another team of horses. A logging operation with horses is just a little bit easier than with a tractor. Horses, you hitch them on to a log, and they'll pull till they get tired, then stop and rest, then loosen the log. A horse is quite a knowing animal. With a machine you've got to do it all.

Your horses last about eighteen to twenty years. The oxen will last twelve to fourteen. But when you're done with that team of horses, they're good for dog food, or you can bury them. That yoke of cattle, when you're done with them, you've got beef. Last year, when we were sugaring, I had been down to Delair's slaughterhouse and seen a Holstein bull that didn't weigh as much as either one of my oxen. He brought nearly $800 for beef. Well, that was a terrific price. I told the boys, "Be careful with those fellows; they're worth more for beef than they are for sugaring."

Just the same, why sell them? If you sell them, you've got to pay the government. You have to operate so as not to pay the government. If you get any money ahead, you want to buy land or cattle or machinery —something that's solid, something that's secure. I like to feel that I'm pretty secure—keep out of debt and buy only what I need and try to live right off the farm.

I've always got a lot of planting I want to do. I'll put in quite a few potatoes. If the potatoes are cheap in the spring, farmers won't plant them. The next year the price will be sky-high. Lot of times I can buy potatoes a whole lot cheaper than I can raise them, but, just the same, you got the land: you want to get in there and plant. Just the same with the pig business: if I see a lot of them are raising pigs, well, I don't have too many. I've got eight sows that'll have piggies. Two years ago I had fourteen sows, and I was the only one around that had any pigs.

When they say you can make farmers, you can't. They can read all the storybooks on farming they want, but a born farmer is brought right up in it. You have to like it, and you have to stay with it. You can't say, "Well, I'm going to Florida this winter—to heck with everything." Because it would be to heck with everything. These farms don't run themselves. They're just like a wheelbarrow: it doesn't go anywhere unless you're pushing it.

THE VITALITY OF WALTER SMITH'S FARM, *with acreage extending into the towns of Marshfield, Plainfield and East Montpelier, appears to belie the statistics of the disappearing Vermont farm. Both Walter and Donald Johnson, whose tidy, spacious farm sits on Knob Hill, continue to ship milk from their Holstein herds every other day. But Eunice Gray lives with her husband, Max, in a farmhouse retired from farming. Both "work out"—Eunice as a secretary at Goddard College, Max as a dairy inspector for the Cabot Creamery. Although a few other working farms inhabit the landscape, they struggle against twentieth-century change with the stubbornness of a minority.*

## Eunice Gray, 58

I can remember when I first came to visit and stay all night up on the farm. I came in February, right after a snowstorm. The trees were white and lopped down with snow. I thought it was the most beautiful setting I ever saw. If you go away and come back, you say, "I don't know as we saw any prettier country than right here."

The house was always nicely kept—not extravagant, but everything in its place. Max's father had died when he was eleven. His mother kept house for the grandfather. She really wanted to leave. That meant the place would be ours. At the time you don't think of those things— one day followed another—but you look back and see that conditions were right.

When we were first married, we bought a team of horses. Max used them for several years on the farm and to work in the woods in the wintertime. I came home from the hospital with my first daughter in a horse and buggy in 1939. It was mud season—April. You just didn't go with anything but a horse.

You had to carry a kerosene lamp from one room to the other, and a lantern to the barn to do chores. We had electricity put in in 1939. In the barn, electricity meant milking machines and water pumps. Water was gravity-fed before. We didn't have a bathroom in the house until '47. We had a two-holer on the end of the house, 'way to the further end of the woodshed. Every room had what we called vessels, pots, slop pails. Part of your daily routine was emptying the pots and washing them, along with filling the lamps and trimming the wicks.

You washed on Monday, ironed on Tuesday, baked on Wednesday. You mixed this along in with your cleaning. Max's mother felt that you had to do dust-mopping and dusting every day. You know the amount of ash that flies in the air from wood stoves. You always had socks to darn. I had five children, and I worked out with Max when we didn't have a hired man. My mother would come up and get me caught up on my mending.

Back in 1938 and '39 you didn't cook the unusual foods you cook nowadays, but neither did you have the packaged foods. At our place, potato and meat was typical. We always dressed our own beef and pork, pickled our hams, made salt pork and smoked meat ourselves. We didn't have a freezer. We'd leave meat out to freeze, and then store it in a little building partway between the house and the barn so no animals could get to it.

When we first started farming, we sold cream instead of milk. You separated it at home and sold the cream to the creamery to make into butter. Then we started selling milk in cans. Max always kept track of the number of pounds of milk each cow gave, morning and night. The more milk they gave, the more profit. You were paid on the amount of butterfat in the milk.

He would empty the milk from the milking machine into a pail. I would pick it up and carry it to the milk room and weigh it, write down the amount and dump it. With two machines going, it was constant back and forth. I'd also do whatever chores needed to be done — feed the cows, clean the gutters, clean calf pens.

Then you had to have a bulk tank in the milk room. The changeover was a terrific expense. This is one reason a lot of farmers stopped sending milk. Max's health was very bad at the time of the changeover, which is why we stopped making milk altogether. We sold the dairy cows and just kept heifers.

Max had a hankering to grow such things as blueberries and strawberries and raspberries, but he didn't have time to do those extras. When he sold the dairy herd, he started doing more gardening. He has three fabulous gardens now. The garden was never my responsibility. I never had to feel that I was to do the hoeing or the weeding. I was more likely to mow lawns.

I don't feel old, but such a great change has taken place in our lifetime. We don't neighbor several times a week like we used to. Now people do things with the people they work with. Most people are new people, anyway. They come and go so fast. We stayed put. There are not too many of those people left.

DRIVING TO DONALD AND PAULINE JOHNSON'S FARM *was the first time I'd ever been on this back road opposite Knob Hill Pond. At the house a cat sat on the steps, but no one answered the door. I walked to the long, large barn and entered through the milk house. Mrs. Johnson glanced at me, then asked me to stop the calf about to run out the open end of the barn. I didn't know how to stop a calf. She chased around a couple of calves while her husband remained at the far end of the barn. I had the impression they didn't know who I was. Just as I was about to introduce myself, Mrs. Johnson said her husband would be right with me—they'd had a busy morning cleaning the barn. I followed her into the house. Mr. Johnson joined us shortly.*

## Donald and Pauline Johnson, 52 and 48

PAULINE: She wants to make a book, you see, of things that's gone by.

LINDA: Would you like to talk about the farm?

DONALD: You wanna buy it? (Chuckles)

LINDA: Is it for sale?

DONALD: Why, shore! You can sell anything that you can get money enough out of.

LINDA: Are you serious? Really?

PAULINE: He's done that all his life. He was born here in this bedroom, right where my kitchen is. He's been here for fifty-two years, so I don't think he'd like to part with it.

DONALD: I was here. Been here all my life. My father and my brother owned the farm. My father, he always growed two, three acres of potatoes and had his thirty, forty cows. He cut his wood to heat his place with and sell a little, and always had a hundred, two hundred hens. If things didn't go too good in the barn, maybe the eggs would be up. It was diversified farming where they didn't rely on just one thing for an income.

After I bought, times had changed over. You put on an extra twenty cows and just tended to them. I built on my garage and built on my bunker silo, and my calf barn out back I built on. The only way that I shall go along is stick right to my barn full of cattle. Most of my fields are small and rough—rolling, put it that way.

With farming you got to expand until you can pay your bills. Farmers need more supplementary income until things pick up or get worse—one or the other—or they're going to have to sell out. It wouldn't have took but a little bit more, and I'd had to sold out.

I pulled my wrist off in a forage wagon one Saturday night. I had just come home from running the roads. The wind was blowing; it was cold there in the first of October. I changed my clothes and went right to the barn. In my tractor cab were my big leather mittens. They had been wet and were hard as a board.

It was a catching of that chunk of leather mitten that pulled my hand away. I tried to unhook my mitten, but it yanked me terrifically hard and rolled that wrist right off in two seconds. It chewed my arm all up into hamburg. I shut my machine off and come to the house and put on a tourniquet.

The doctor stuffed it all back together and sewed it up. Then he put the antibiotic to me. The doctor, he sat on my bed and didn't want me to worry about his bills. He talked to me real strong to keep my mind

off what was going to happen in the future. He didn't know what I had to home, or whether I was all right financially.

The thing that sticks out the most, compared to the hurt, was that next morning when they brought me in a little bowl of broth and some tea and some toast. They wound me up in bed, and I reached right over and grabbed that spoon with my left hand. I don't know how to word it, but to pick up that spoon was a feeling that will always, always stay with me as long as I live.

Yauh, I come left-handed right off quick now, by gosh. I got lots of friends, of course, and they all come to see me and sent me cards. But them cards, on the back side I would practice. I wanted to know how to grab out my checkbook and write out a check left-handed.

I was gone for a month in the hospital. I was glad to come home. It's quite a feeling to take off in a hurry, not knowing as you'd ever come back. I got to build back up now. No way of knowing how big I'll get or if I'll sell off. It all depends on how I come along.

*The character of the Vermont landscape has changed radically. What was here when pioneers first came doesn't resemble anything that's here today. The biggest change has been the rise and fall of farming. You can't appreciate it, but at one time probably eighty percent of Vermont was cleared for farming. You can go back on some of these hillsides, miles from nowhere, and run into cellar holes and old barns. It just staggers your imagination. You can't imagine anybody would farm these areas of rock and ledge and swamp and north-facing slopes. Right now, probably eighty percent of the land is back into forest.* — BILL MOULTON

ALTHOUGH THE CHARACTERISTIC SHAPE *of rounded hills and abrupt ridges descending towards narrow river valleys remains, land use changes. Where property used to be an accurate measure of wealth—what the land could produce in crops, animals, woodlot and sugarbush—acreage no longer reflects what the taxpayer can contribute to maintain a town and its school.*

*David Codling is one of four listers employed by the town of Marshfield to evaluate property on which the grand list is based. On a hot summer day we talked in the kitchen of his new, small house—"I cut down on my square footage as much as I could to cut my taxes." David Codling, who lives across the road from his brother, Tinker, is a security guard at I.B.M. in Essex Junction, a daily round-trip drive of 100 miles.*

## David Codling, 36

I couldn't tell you right offhand what the total acreage of Marshfield is. Over the years actual acreage has never been written down. Everything's been put in as "more or less." Most generally, it would run less.

Now, when anything is subdivided, they have got to have a survey. Right now, we have 620 homes, about fifty percent old and fifty percent new. We have 75 to 80 trailers.

Appraising a home is all done on a grading system. The State sets the figures. It goes 2, 4, 6, 8, 10. Most of the homes around this area are average, about a "6" grade. They would have probably a thousand square feet of living space. Most have three bedrooms. Most use sheetrock on the walls. Lately, they are carpeting floors; you don't see too much hardwood floor anymore. The old foundations were stone; today it's all concrete.

A good many of your old farmhouses where people have lived all their lives will hit lower grades. A lot have been bought'n up and remodeled and are graded higher, but the biggest share are in real bad shape. The old plastered walls have dried out over the years. Your floors are those wide, soft, wood boards. The kitchens are no way near modern like they are today with dishwashers and garbage disposals.

The State says you shouldn't be living in a home with over fifty percent depreciation. We've got only two: the plaster's off the walls, they don't have any furniture, there are rags in the windows. Homes don't depreciate too fast now because property is climbing every year. The cost of building a home goes up. Of all the new homes we appraised this year, not a one was finished. They ran out of money. This isn't good in a community.

You've got to look at the simple fact of income right in this location. The average income is probably $5,000. We had a place sell to a doctor in New York. The acreage price was real high. This automatically jumped the value of our land sales. We aren't able to stand up to what this fellow can pay. It's going to drive us off our land.

In the surrounding communities, land is selling higher than in Marshfield. We feel it's because we've got so much land that lies back where you can't get at it, except for walking. It's mostly good for growing trees. Otherwise, it isn't developed in any way. It's dead weight that other people are paying the tax load on.

I feel you've got to develop this land and make it pay for itself. We should have some kind of industry. We could build a furniture factory. It wouldn't cause too much pollution, and you have plenty of timber around here. If we had an industry that would offer jobs to go along *with* the property owner, it would help.

Mainly, what we've got left is two or three filling stations and a couple of stores. Our farms are pretty well depleted. You can't tax them much heavier, or they aren't going to be around. We have a total number of seven operating farms. That's counting Berte's egg farm. Along the river from Marshfield to Plainfield is all good farmland. It's flat, about the flattest stuff we've got—no stones. What have we got there for operating farms? One, where there used to be twelve. This land is all being broke up. It'll never be going back into farms.

Land stood for years and years and years at $30 an acre. It was never evaluated. Thirty dollars an acre didn't run up any tax money. We weren't growing. We had our own schools which didn't cost anything. It was always slow living up here. The land was so cheap that people came in and paid outrageous amounts of money for it. The State started setting educational standards. Now everything's expanded to the point where we're trying to grow too fast.

The biggest share of your tax dollar goes into education. The State said, "New schools," so we had new schools. We didn't buy a school; we bought a million-dollar business. We're throwing our money away, you might as well say, if we're going to educate our kids just to go out of state and work. People wouldn't holler half as much if they felt, "My kid's got an education. He can step into a nice job around here and help support the school *with* his education."

Every year we have what we call a Grievance Day. If a person feels they're unjustly used, as far as their appraisal, they come and meet with the listers. This year the complaints made you sick. You felt just as bad as the person grieving. But what could you do? Just because they were on a fixed income or not making as much money, you can't show partiality. You were using everybody equal.

MAHLON WHITCOMB'S SINGLE POINT OF REFERENCE *is the land. Bitterness towards those who misuse the land has grown over time: "They're trying to live without the land today. If nobody works this land, we're all going to starve to death. If the government don't wake up and help the farmers, they cannot survive." With his second wife, Louine, Mahlon lives in a narrow trailer at the end of a long driveway. From every window he has a view of the fields and woods he worked since coming to the hill in 1938. In Hebrew, "Mahlon" means "pining."*

## Mahlon Whitcomb, 55

I've been here two-thirds of my life. This was my father-in-law's farm. Then it went to my first wife. I was milkin' twenty-five cows by hand. We had to cool our milk with ice. We used to cut big blocks up there to Knob Hill Pond. The ice house was behind the milk house. The man who was gatherin' the milk had to lug the big milk cans to the road in the winter.

We had a $10,000 mortgage on the farm. They come here and tell us we had to have a bulk tank and fancy milkhouses. That would add another $5,000 or $10,000 to our debt. You couldn't make that much milk on a small farm. We had to quit. That's why all these farms are gone today. My first wife was sick with cancer. That cost about $10,000.

Three years ago Louine and I sold the house and six acres, which left us roughly seventy acres. Now we're being forced out of the rest. I don't want to sell this land, but I have no other way. With these high taxes you can't own land. I can't find a job to earn the money. We are eligible for food stamps, but we don't want to go on welfare.

This land is valuable to me because I spent my life here workin' it. If

I sell it, what have I got left? I've got nothin'. I don't even have a tree left. It's like livin' in a damn city. All my rights and everything I've got is gone. My life's work is a mobile home and a garage and a few little acres.

The hill has changed in so many ways that it's hard to describe. There's none of the same people that were here when I came. Everybody has died or moved away. Today, who do you know? They come and they go. I am the last one on Hollister Hill.

The out-of-staters are pushin' the Vermonters off the land. People are comin' into this state because it's a rat race in the city. Here, it's peaceful. They can walk around and hear themselves talk. They live different, and they believe different. They don't farm or do any type of work like we used to. They have all these new methods of farmin'. You can't tell them anything, even you've been a farmer all your life. They'd rather believe somebody in a white shirt behind a desk at the university.

The women are different. I don't believe in the women's lib. If a woman's workin' on the same job 'side of a man, I expect and believe that she should have the same pay. But I don't think that they should take over construction work, because a woman is not rugged enough. By the time they get forty, they're not going to look like women anymore.

It's a new world, actually. Too many people don't want to earn their livin'. Back twelve, fifteen years ago, when there was all kinds of work, you'd see young men with ribbons tied around their hair, livin' on food stamps. They wouldn't work. That's when the damn government should have cut out the food-stamp business. Now they are tryin' to cut it out—now, when you need it.

Nixon and Watergate are what got us where we are now. Everything was thrown in one pot, as you might say. People weren't watchin' what was happenin' to the rest of the country. We all know that Nixon wasn't interested in the country. How he ever got in the second time is more than I'll ever know.

Politicians are two people. When they are runnin', they are one; when they are in, they don't know you anymore. They are not for the people. They are only for themselves. We should have somebody that's lived poor get into the White House. The rich overrun the poor. Why?

Today a handful of people in government is runnin' the whole thing. We have no say anymore. It's the same with this land. This land don't even belong to us. We pay taxes on it. That's all. I can't even sell this piece of land without a zoning permit. Is that freedom?

ALTHOUGH ART KRUEGER'S GRANDFATHERS *were born in Europe, his parents met and married in Connecticut. Art's hope for the future is that people will voluntarily correct the wrongs done to the American landscape, particularly to agricultural land: "Land has to go back to small holders, but not holders who can sell their land. We've been working for a long time now on organizing a land trust in Vermont. If we can get, say, five percent of the land in the state in a land trust, we will act as a brake on the market system."*

## Art Krueger, 30

How did I get to Vermont? Well, by car! I was in graduate school at the University of Rhode Island. At that time I was getting very interested in the ecological movement. That summer, while hiking in the White Mountains of New Hampshire, I saw a beer can. What's this world coming to? Coming down off the mountains, there was one continuous neon sign, and ski areas, and businesses advertising—sell, sell—and it was ugly. New Hampshire's basically a very beautiful place, but it's been uglified. Connecticut's basically a very beautiful place, but it's been uglified. The only place that was interested in doing anything about it was Vermont.

I happen to have a degree in Sanitary Engineering, so I started applying for jobs in the New England States and in the Northwest. The first job that opened up was in Water Resources in Vermont, and I took it. I started to live in a hunting camp with a friend. There was a dichotomy of living in the country and working in the city of Montpelier. It was driving me nuts.

While still working for the State, the war in Vietnam came more and more into my mind. Finally, in the spring of '72, I found myself protesting the war in front of the Plainfield Post Office with the hippies of Goddard College. That was the beginning of change inside myself. Two months later I quit my job. I started going all over Vermont to get people to vote for George McGovern because that seemed the best thing to do at the time.

After the election I was exhausted. Since I had some money, I took a trip. This was my first foray out into other parts of the country in some ten years. I was really amazed. Since then, all the billboards had gone up in Ohio, which used to be very beautiful country — the way that land rolls! It's just commercialized garbage all the way out to Indiana. And places like Indianapolis, oh, God help us. When I came back to Vermont, the mountains had grown at least a thousand feet taller, and I said, "Jesus! I want to live here."

I was brought up as a Catholic, but that summer I became a convinced Quaker. "Thou shalt not kill" is very important. Paying taxes is the equivalent of killing in this country. I never filed an income tax for that year. I didn't know if I owed them or if they owed me. Living in a rural lifestyle, you never earn enough money to contribute a thousand dollars a year for the government to build bombs.

I've been thinking that a lot of things are obviously very wrong with America. I don't want to do any of those bad things. I will do something constructive with my life. Well, what's wrong? One wrong thing is land ownership. You shouldn't be able to take farmland

and plow it wrong to erode the topsoil, or use chemicals to destroy the soil, or strip-mine it, or pave it.

The land's been around for an infinite period of time — millions and millions and millions of years. It's absurd for us, who live at most eighty years, to say, "This is my land." Land ownership in America is very tenuous. If you go back to find out how the land got given out, they say, "Somebody owned it." Wait a second. Where'd they get it? The land has all been extorted or stolen or somewhat taken from the Indians. They probably took it by a very nasty means from other Indians.

In Vermont we have this very curious thing of the Governor of New Hampshire giving Vermont away to some rich friends of his — Ethan Allen was one — and the Governor of New York giving away the same land. Well, I'd like to know who gave it to them. The king? Well, then, where did the king get it? I mean, he got it from God? Since we don't have the king anymore — we got rid of him — maybe we ought to get rid of this land-ownership structure. The bank owns most of our land. As soon as we see ourselves clear of the mortgage, we will definitely want to put it into a land trust.

When one man holds a lot of land, a lot of men hold no land. So I've been thinking about how much land's enough. When I first came to Vermont, I needed a hundred acres. You have to have at least a hundred acres to get away from it all. I mellowed out considerably when I found out if you own a hundred acres you have to pay a lot of taxes. I now have just the house and eight acres. That's more or less what you need to live on anyway.

VOICES FROM MID AUGUST — *Kitty Brown's again, on berrying, catsup-making, and the state of the world.*

## Kitty Brown, 44

I am not a farmer by birth. I am a village gal from Cabot. My dad had a few cattle and a barn in the village, but to live on the farm itself, no. My mother'd play around with a few chickens up until the time of her death.

My husband's mother passed away when he was just five years old. My mother passed away when I was eleven years old. I couldn't have any knowledge from my mother 'cause she left us too soon. My sister-in-law that lived on the home farm was, shall you say, an ordinary person, but an awful lot of knowledge come from her. I think anybody should learn the basic way to survive. All this really generates right back to that, doesn't it?

This is my father-in-law's old homestead. He's now eighty-seven. He bought it from his dad in 1927. My husband's brother now owns the farm. It's getting kind of broken up. We hope there won't be any more breakage, but you can't never tell.

It was different twenty-five years ago. You did raise your own things. Your farmers had the surplus. You could go up on my father-in-law's garden and pick a bushel of produce and take it home and can it. He'd just give it away.

He raised chickens. If some of his children come along, he'd say, "You want a chicken to eat for Sunday?" Chop the head off and think nothing of it — didn't cost him a cent. Now your farmers might have enough for themselves, but feed costs so much that they won't give away as much as they used to.

We always had our apples. We picked them up bushel after bushel. It seems like we had so much, if one didn't look just right we could drop it in the garbage. Today, we might eat the core to pay for the price.

Back then, the family picked berries galore. After we got the chores done in the morning, we'd say, "Well, it's a good day to go berrying," so we'd pack a lunch and away we'd go. We'd spend, oh, five or six hours picking berries.

The biggest year we put down 1400 quarts down-cellar. That was in 1949. We had all these tomatoes, and we said, "We've made everything but catsup." We was going to set out to make catsup. Well, that was all right.

We got all the ingredients on the stove, but it needed the vinegar. The last morning we were doing some haying. My husband came in from the barn and he says, "Are you going out and rake the hay?" And I said, "Yes," I said, "but it's almost time for this vinegar to go in. Well, ten minutes won't make any difference. I guess I'll put the vinegar in." I left it on the stove to simmer.

My sister-in-law lived in an adjoining apartment in the house. She and I were making catsup together. 'Course my father-in-law could cook as well as any woman. I'm sure that I told him to tell her that I'd put the vinegar in, but I guess he didn't hear me 'cause he was getting older. God bless his soul, he helped us so much that we forgive him for this little mistake.

Anyway, she come out after I'd left and she said, "Do you think Kitty put the vinegar in that catsup?" And my father-in-law says, "No, I don't think so," he says, "there's some setting there," and, shore enough, she adds the vinegar, so it got a double dose. We bottled it up and used it all, but that's the only time we tried catsup.

People used to look after each other years ago, more than they do today. You might call up the neighbor and say, "Hey, Don, you want to come over and help me today?" And the farmer'd say, "Yuh, I'll be over." Then you would switch back and to for whatever he wanted. It wasn't money, money, money all the time.

Today you're living in a different kind of a world. You take my own case. I was working out forty hours a week as a nurse's aid in a nursing home. At night I would be tired. My father-in-law was getting bed-ridden. If he was taken sick, my sister would call and I'd go over. Not that I begrudge him an ounce of my time.

Then my sister's baby was born, and I was taken sick with a kidney infection, so the decision was made to put him in a nursing home. You'd faint right over if I told you the price. We didn't ever thought any of us would live long enough to see the day 'cause we've always taken care of our own family.

We were home people and didn't have jobs like we do now. All my sister-in-laws work out. I don't think it was their own choice. It came because they didn't have the surplus money. Sometimes they like their job, but they wished they could stay to home. Due to the high cost of living, I don't think that they can. You hear a grumbling or a griping. The women get so tired out, they don't know if they're coming or going. That's what it all generates to.

BECAUSE HER PARENTS ARE DIVORCED, *Margaret Krueger comes from Connecticut each summer to visit her father, Art Krueger. Art lives with Carlene Lindgren, whom he plans to marry shortly, as well as with her two children, Kate, six, and Chris, five. Margaret is tall, with long, straight, light hair, and admits to looking mostly like her mother. A summer outdoors has transformed her skin from winter-pale to freckled, brown and peeling.*

## Margaret Krueger, 7

LINDA: How long have you been here this summer?

MARGARET: Six weeks.

LINDA: Why are you here for six weeks?

MARGARET: I had to visit my father.

LINDA: Did you have to, or did you want to?

MARGARET: I had to.

LINDA: Why do you have to visit him?

MARGARET: Because he doesn't live with us. That's why.

LINDA: Does he ever visit you?

MARGARET: Yes! Sometimes. Not very often.

LINDA: Do you like coming here?

MARGARET: Nm-hm, because after a while I get to miss my mother, and it gets boring, and I have to be with Kate and Chris. Sometimes they fight, and sometimes they even really hurt somebody. It's hard for me to go through it, but I do.

LINDA: But you like to see your dad, don't you?

MARGARET: Yeahuh!

LINDA: Do you miss your dad when you're home?

MARGARET: No. That's a funny thing. When I'm here, I miss my mom, but when I'm down there, I don't miss my dad.

LINDA: Do you feel that some day this would be your home?

MARGARET: No.

LINDA: Would you like it if your mom were here?

MARGARET: Yes!

LINDA: Is it the place or the people you're with that's really important?

MARGARET: The place *and* the people that I'm with.

LINDA: Do you think you'd be happy anyplace your mom would be?

MARGARET: Yes.

LINDA: Why do you like it more at home?

MARGARET: It's more exciting. I can go play with my really nice friends. I can ride my bike, and I don't have a bike here. I can go downtown, and I can't go downtown here. I can buy anything I want if I have the right amount of money, but here I'm not allowed. It's funner at home than it is here.

LINDA: Did anything good happen this summer?

MARGARET: Um-hm. Now I know how to swim, and last year I didn't. My father's teaching me.

LINDA: Did anything else good happen this summer?

MARGARET: Not going to school!

LINDA: What's happening tomorrow that you're looking forward to?

MARGARET: Going home! My mother's going to pick me up.

LINDA: How do you go back and forth, usually?

MARGARET: I go on the train all the way to my aunt's in Boston, and then she puts me on the bus to go all the way to Vermont, and then Art picks me up.

LINDA: Do you like traveling by yourself?

MARGARET: It's okay.

LINDA: What do you do when you're sitting by yourself?

MARGARET: I think about things.

LINDA: How old are you now, Margaret?

MARGARET: Seven.

THIS STORY OF MIFF KEENE'S *was recorded at Walter Smith's, in the unnaturally cool downstairs of an old farmhouse, while the August heat outside prompted Miff to comment, "Even God Himself couldn't hay in weather like this."*

## Miff Keene, 53

Well, folks, I've got to tell you about the time I was out in Indiana. We

had a big farm out there in corn country. One Sunday after chores we'd got done hayin', but my wife and I thought we'd take the hand rake and scrape the little scatterin's away from the fence next to the corn. The corn was lookin' pretty thick. So I told Mary, I says, "Why don't we go into the cornfield and see just how high that corn is?"

We went into the cornfield and, my gosh! when you looked up into that corn, it was all dark, just like a coal mine. I couldn't see the sun shine at all. So I took my hand rake by the stail and run the handle up as far as I could reach. I could just touch the bottom leaf on that gosh-darn corn.

Well, I knew sumpin' had to be done because no machinery of mine could ever cut that corn — it had such heavy stalks? I didn't really know just what to do. But Mary told me, she says, "We've got to get some help and get that corn cut."

So I got hold of six Canadian boys from Ontario on the telephone, and they said they'd just as soon come down and help me out. You know what they done? They had three two-man chainsaws with them, and they just throwed them over their backs and swum right down the Great Lakes.

They went to work into that corn, but it was so damn dark in there they had to use miners' lamps to see what they were doin'. When they got to the end of the last row, the last stalk fell across the state border into Illinois. And I'll be damned if I didn't have to ask the State of Illinois if I could go over and get the tassel.

The way it ended up was somethin' like this: we had so darn much corn we just saved the ears. Some of the ears was as long as a log, and we just run them right into the silos. I had seventeen silos, eighteen by ninety-seven feet. The stalks and the leaves I sold to Kellogg's Company for corn flakes.

And that's all on that. How do you like that tale?

JEAN HAWKINS LIVES ON HAWKSTEAD FARM, *at the upper end of East Hill Road in East Calais with her husband, Merle. Their closest neighbors are Paul and Louise Bouchard. Jean's father-in-law bought the farm in 1915, but when she and her husband took it over, it was ready for a sheriff's sale. In spite of hard times the Hawkins have refused to leave: "My husband stays on the farm because this is the family homestead. He never regretted a moment he farmed."*

*During our conversation, Mrs. Hawkins and I sat at the kitchen table with her granddaughter, age four, and infant grandson. She babysits for them while their parents work. Towards the end of the interview, her son came in for a drink of water and gave a sip to his son in the high chair. He was finishing the last haying of summer.*

## Jean Hawkins, 54

My husband and I went alone to Essex Fair the last part of August. It seemed rather strange to go alone. We've always had a bunch of kids and took a picnic lunch. This year we grabbed a grinder and a bottle of pop down there.

This was a family tradition that started out when the kids were real little. We took them to the Lyndonville or Barton Fair, then the grown people took off a day and went to Essex. We only had one day off in those days, so we used to go to the fair. We've missed three years during the war out of the last thirty-four.

I think all farm people like the fair. Usually, we look at the cows, but this year we went to the horse races. My husband's favorite pastime is watching the sulkies race. We bet with each other — no, there isn't any money involved. One thing that interested me is the Vermont build-ing. That's supposed to have things that make your home more livable. I dearly love music, so we went over to where they were demonstratin' electric organs.

I went to see the new trailers while my husband watched horse-pullin'. In the pullin' contest they load a stoneboat till the horses can't pull that weight any further. Myself, I like the tractor-pullin' the best.

My husband was brought up in the days of horses. Back when we started farmin', we did our work with horses. We didn't have a tractor on this farm till 1948. My husband actually put it off just as long as he could. He liked his horses, but they just couldn't keep up with a trac-tor. I think that the older generation of farm people hated to see the era of the horses gone.

We were married in September 1940. My husband milked twenty cows by hand until the followin' December. He had trouble with his hands, so we got our first milkin' machine. Now we have a milkin' parlor, which is even easier, as far as the operator is concerned. Once upon a time we had a dumpin' station, and we thought that was won-derful. Nowadays, your milk goes right through to the bulk tank. It's really interestin' how a generation progresses more than the one before it.

I came here as a bride. We had a three-room apartment upstairs. The water ran gravity-feed. Now we have an electric pump. I always had a washin' machine, but my mother-in-law downstairs had one of those old gasoline-powered Maytags. You had to run your hose out the window so you wouldn't get all the fumes. It ran well if you could get it started.

I often wished that I had had a dryer when my children were little. We had a wood furnace, and diapers got dried over the register. Sometimes they were stiff, which I didn't think too much of. Probably the biggest change in a woman's life is the washer and the dryer and the hot-water tank.

In the 1950's we were milkin' thirty, forty cows and had 400 layers. I spent all weekend when my kids were little grading eggs. Where you have all mechanical grading now, I had a little scale that said: extra-large, large, medium, and small. We shipped ninety dozen eggs a week.

We got the baby chicks in the spring and, just as soon as it warmed up enough, they went onto the top floor of the barn. The three brothers would dress them off from Thanksgiving to just before Christmas. Us girls would pinfeather them and singe them and sew up their neck and tuck them down in and get them ready to go. They took them down to the city and sold them. If I remember right, that was our money to buy the Christmas presents.

Of course, farmin' was a lot less expensive than it is today. Today you handle a lot, but you don't keep it. If you're going to farm, it takes two paychecks. Either the wife has to help on the farm or work out. If you never had any children, maybe you'd make a fairly good livin', but there ain't much point if you don't.

At one time my husband did work out. He had a hired man when the children were little. He worked in North Montpelier in the woolen mill nights, 11:00 to 7:00. Those days we didn't have a school bus, so he took the kids to school. Most mornings it was near 10:00 before he got to bed. He'd get up at 6:00 at night to help milk, then go back to bed until 10:30, then go to work.

That was when we didn't have much money. If he hadn't worked out, we'd have probably lost our farm. It was one of those cases of have-to. When springtime came, he got laid off, then right in the middle of haying, they wanted him back. He couldn't go because the cows had to have feed.

My hubby says he didn't like punchin' the time clock. We milk at 5:00 in the afternoon here, but if we're fifteen minutes late, nobody's goin' to give you the devil and fire you. When a rainy day comes, you can go to the city and do your business, which you couldn't do if you was workin' out. They say there's no money in farmin' now, but, to a certain extent, it's a free life.

This is good corn country up here. As soon as the corn is cut and the snow flies, the farm boys go snowmobilin'. If every farmer could give these boys a bonus, it would make a lot of difference. You've got to have some compensation to offset the long hours a farmer puts in.

Right now we have every third Sunday off, my husband and I. That's not much. We've had more time off because we've been to Florida four times in the last nine years. But I do think young people are migratin' to the city because they just don't like this bein' tied down. You are tied, especially if you haven't got help.

We don't get up as early here probably as we should, but you can't expect a man to be out of the barn 10:00 to 10:30 at night and back in there at 5:00, seven days a week. You're not goin' to find anybody that's goin' to do that. Those days are gone.

# Early Fall

*I just had a great wave of homesickness wash over me in the vision of a blue enamel bowl of Duchess apples on my table at the farm, while the house is fragrant with that early September smell of interminable applesauce (Duchess ripen early). The house would be kind of dim, but outside would be golden and autumn-warm.*

— A LETTER FROM MARY ANDERSON, A NEIGHBOR ON HOLLISTER HILL.

IN SEPTEMBER AND OCTOBER, time is caught in a parenthesis of brief color and light after the first killing frost. Indian summer, it's called, but summer it is not — merely a reprieve from the inevitable. Not only are the top leaves of cucumbers and squashes blackened by the white frost, but whatever was once green is now stunted by the cold. The northwest wind stirs up a dull rustle in gardens, fields and woods.

The solitary walker takes advantage of this small time between summer insects and November hunters to explore the seminal dryness of an autumn field. Brown-eyed Susans are bent over and brushy with small seeds. Thin bees cling to a few clumps of late goldenrod. The field clover, once a quaint purple, is now dark and dead. Split milkweed pods deposit their floating seeds on any breeze.

Tasting neither sour nor sweet, soft nor hard, an apple from a scabby tree fits perfectly within the hand. In the dry leaves of encroaching woods, a chipmunk sounds as big as a dog, a dog as big as a deer. The soft stutter of crickets is a reminder to turn homeward before the chilling dusk.

On a fine afternoon we can "put the garden to bed" for the next six months. After chopping the dried cornstalks, there is pleasure in watching flies suck the last sweetness. Before dark, a neighbor covers her dahlias with old blankets. We welcome the last diversion of "leaf-peepers," whose admiration of the colored leaves does not include what their brilliance portends. We want a fire at night and early in the morning to "take the chill off."

Soon we will descend towards November; beyond that waits an abiding winter. If the remaining half of the year is tinged with the unreality of brief time, we can soon relax: in winter there's all the time in the world. The wheel will turn again to lodge in its old, familiar position. The brake will be set. There is no escape. We are caught in the long reality. Whatever work remains, remains unfinished. Where you are, you belong.

THE FIRST DAY OF FALL *begins the morning after Labor Day, when schoolchildren wait on Hollister Hill Road for the yellow bus. It passes two former one-room schoolhouses, remnants of the rural education abandoned as late as the 1940's in central Vermont.*

*At the top of the first long ascent up Hollister Hill stands a Victorian house, called haunted by children and their parents. However, the house has never seen a ghost. In fact, an earlier barn had what is called locally a "spring" floor, which made it ideal for country dances.*

*In 1943 Marge and Vernon Newton, Sr., bought the farm through the Federal Land Bank. Like an ancient maple surrounded by young saplings, "the big house" has spawned family-inhabited trailers and new houses on*

*either side. The Newtons live in the closest trailer. Marge Newton recalls*
*attending one-room schools while growing up in nearby towns.*

## Marge Newton, 64

In my family there was two girls and four boys growin' up. We lived
on a farm in Middlesex. In the fall you buy everybody new shoes and
stockin's for school. They weren't socks then, they were stockin's.
You know how warm it is in September. We had to walk a mile and
eight-tenths to get to school. After I get out of sight of the house, I'd
take off my shoes and stockin's and hide them in the stone wall and go
to school barefeet.

My mother had a fit. How she happened to know was one time we
got caught in the rain, and my shoes weren't wet. Another time was
early in the spring when the June roses — those wild roses you see on
the road? — bloom. We were going to take the teacher a bouquet.
Someone said, "We'll get thorns." So big me went in barefeet and got
a thorn in my big toe. That let the cat out o' the bag. I had to wear
shoes after that for a while.

The first school I went to was Shady Rill School. You don't know
how a country school is. There was twenty-six of us, first to eighth
grade, of all kinds and colors and dispositions. There was only one
teacher. It all depended on how much discipline she had. The teacher
would ring the bell, and you'd have to line up in the anteroom, they
called it. You had to come in real quiet and take your seat.

Her whole front would be her first grade, then her second grade,
and then the older ones would sit in the back. Now, if you're in the
eighth grade, and you're a boy, and you're a little bit on the bully side
anyway, oh, just knock those little kids left and right, it don't matter.
Sometimes bully boys would use slingshots and shoot little stones or
dried peas and beans. You had to look out for yourself. If you didn't,
you just got tromped on, that's all.

The girls did teasin' and pickin': "Oh, your dress isn't made right," or "You got a rubber band on your hair today. Where's your hair ribbon?" Pick, pick, pick. 'Course, back then we wore hair ribbons and long hair. I had curls, and the kids'd pull 'em.

When we went to the Middlesex Center School, there was a lot o' brush 'side o' the road, y'know, over the stone wall? We'd go out there to eat our lunch when it was warm. We had our dinner pails—they were lard pails, never a lunch bag, because it'd always come to pieces before you could get to school.

Back then, lunches weren't as they are now. You would have, maybe, homemade bread—you never had store bread—and butter and a hard-boiled egg. Just to be funny you'd crack it on the other guy's head. We'd have some homemade cookie or a piece o' cake. Maybe the next day, or the next day but one, they'd be these birds and squirrels and chipmunks that would come.

We never had any Thermos bottle like they have now. We had nothing to drink till we got back into the schoolhouse. Then we had a cup of water. We'd go to the neighbor's and get a pail o' water that'd sit on this shelf. After a while they discontinued that pail business and had this great big urn. It had a faucet that you'd push and hold these flat paper drinking cups under.

The big kids had to get the water. There were some nice Negro people lived near the school. This father and mother got out of this slavery thing. You could see the welts on the father's back where he had been whipped. And that mother, she had white hair and was the dearest old lady. Back then if you had custard pie, that was something. She used to make these great big thick custard pies with butternuts.

They had this nice clean little tub that the spring water ran into from up in the pasture someplace. And she'd say, "Now, let me wash your pail." She'd go to the reservoir—to the old cook range, y'know—and she'd get the hot water, and she'd wash the pail and the dipper with soap and water. And then she'd take the tea kettle, and she'd put boilin' water all around. And then we'd dip up the water out of this barrel. In the meantime we either got a little slab of this pie or a great big molasses cookie.

And they had apples, a great big nice apple orchard. The edge of it came right on the playground. "Go get apples, go get apples. Have all the apples you want." We never touched their apples. We'd rather gang up and go up on another guy's land and get apples 'cause he'd holler at us and say, "Stay out of there."

ALTHOUGH THE *Twinfield Union School District provides a standard elementary and secondary education to its students, Plainfield is also the home of Goddard College. A native of the area, Tim Pitkin, whose first name is really Royce, retired from the presidency of Goddard in 1969.*

## Tim Pitkin, 73

I was not named, as some people thought, for Josiah Royce, but for a boy in Sioux Falls, South Dakota. My family lived in South Dakota for about seven years. One of my brothers had a playmate whose first name was Royce. I was not born there, but, when they were casting around for names some years later, they dredged up Royce. If you go back to the persons who are my age with whom I grew up in Marshfield, about half of them call me Royce. In recent years, persons who've known me most closely have called me Tim.

I can remember the incident that led to it. I must have been about five years old. I remember my mother singing the song "Timothy Tucker Sings for His Supper." She went to calling me Timothy Tucker. I thought I'd hurt my mother's feelings by saying I didn't like it. I said to her later, "Well, you can call me Timothy Tucker if you want to."

At the same time other members of my family called me "Bug," which apparently went back to the time when I crawled around as a very small child. That name stuck, I must say, for years. When I graduated from Marshfield High School in 1916, some of my classmates were still calling me "Bug." Some of them would now, I guess, if they saw me.

I stayed out of school for two years after I graduated from Marshfield and worked on the farm, as all my brothers had done before me. Except they worked longer. It was common when my oldest brother was around for boys to stay until they were twenty-one. They were a distinct economic asset. I stayed until I was seventeen and then went to Goddard Seminary.

It was just assumed in my family that if you were going away to school, you'd go to Goddard. My own family had been associated with Goddard from the very beginning. My great-grandmother was involved in getting it going. My grandfather was on the Board of Trustees. My father went there; my aunts went there; all of my brothers went there. Keep in mind that the seminary was not a training school for the ministry, but simply a secondary school. They were generally referred to as preparatory schools. Goddard Seminary was started as a preparatory school for Tufts College. Tufts was a Universalist College. My father's family was Universalist.

Although I graduated from the College of Agriculture at the University of Vermont, I did a good bit of work in education. I suppose this was family influence. My oldest brother had quite an influence on me educationally — in other ways, too, for that matter. He tended to be looking forward and finding new ways of doing things. I went to teaching my first year out of college in Plymouth, New Hampshire. I worked like the dickens that year. I taught physics — I had never had a college course in physics — chemistry, biology, and this course in American Social Problems, it was called.

I remember talking with the Registrar at the University of Vermont about my students that might come to the University. I said they'd had this course in Social Problems. He said, "I'll tell you something.

Don't call it 'Social Problems.' Just call it 'Civics.' " I said, "Why?" "Social Problems" didn't have respectability and wasn't hoary with age, but "Civics" was. I thought that was good advice; I've thought of it lots of times since. It's the *name* that's important, not the content, if you want something accepted in certain places.

I learned a tremendous amount from my first year of teaching. I had a very conservative principal, but a very effective one. But I knew that

I wanted to do something else. In one's earlier years you tend to move by ambition. I tried to go on and be a principal myself.

Helen and I got married the end of our first year out of college. We took a job up in Hyde Park, Vermont. She was going to teach English, and I was principal and teaching science. We were much interested in helping kids get along more successfully. We discovered that our usual conventional methods didn't work so well. We began to cast around for ways of improving.

We were in Hyde Park two years, and we liked the town. But I got ambitious and thought I ought to have a bigger school. An opening came up in this bigger school in Groveton, New Hampshire. It was a mill town. There's a different ethos in a mill town. The churches were not churches I was familiar with. I felt like kind of a foreigner.

In the winter of 1926 I had the measles, of all things. And was I sick?! I was practically out of my mind. It took me a *long* time to recover. I decided to quit the school business. I had no job, but we weren't worried. We had this farm up here, the Levi Pitkin Farm. Helen and I set out raspberries and blackberries that year. But as I got to feel better, I decided to go back into school work. I took a job in Wallingford, Vermont. I was there four years.

Then the Depression broke. I decided I'd better get a doctorate if I was going to get one. We went down to Columbia University in New York. I had to borrow money, but we weren't worried about a living. We always figured, "If worse comes to worse, we can get back here on the good old farm." Having the land to fall back on gives you a sense of security. It makes a tremendous difference in the outlook of a person.

My educational experience was in public schools, until I went to Goddard in the fall of 1935 to start a junior college for women. This came about in a curious way. I finished up the work for my doctorate in educational administration in 1932. I was much impressed by William Kilpatrick's and John Dewey's approach to education. I had intended to be a superintendent of schools. I landed up in New London, New Hampshire, where I saw at first hand the junior-college idea.

In February 1935, I decided I'd leave New London because they elected a chap to the school board that was very conservative educationally. I thought, "I wonder if they ever thought of having a junior college at Goddard." A study had recommended that they develop one, but they'd done nothing about it. Goddard had fallen on hard times, as many other private schools had.

At the end of my first year there, the principal decided to get married. I was made the head of the school. I taught, as well as being director. I left the science field and went to teaching social sciences. The second year I was there, we called it Goddard Seminary *and* Junior College.

To show you how naive I was, I figured all you had to do was let people know you've got a junior college, and the girls would come in. What *really* happened was I finally landed one student. I can see her today. She was a very nice-looking blonde girl who was interested in art. Then I thought, "What the heck am I going to do if she's the only one that shows up?" But we kept trying and wound up with this group of twenty-five. We gave the Associate Degree. It has to be said we were a moderately progressive conventional school.

We had a series of faculty meetings to talk about what we could do to improve our teaching. In addition, we began thinking about moving. The City of Barre had grown up around the school. The buildings were not the great buildings that I remembered as a boy. The five-story main building was a great fire hazard — open stairwells from the top clear through to the bottom. You could stand at the top and spit right down to the basement.

We decided to develop a new program to meet the needs of kids of that particular era. We had a meeting at Columbia with Dr. Kilpatrick as the chairman. We put together the proposal for a new institution. We said that all our ideas had been tried out, but they hadn't been brought together in one institution. I remember Dr. Kilpatrick asking us, "Are the bars all down, or are there certain limitations?" My reply was, "The only limitation is that we don't have any money."

Having been in this area, I knew about the Greatwood Farm in Plainfield. It happened that a few years before this period we're talking about, which is now 1938, the owner had died. His wife tried to run the farm and couldn't make ends meet. She decided to sell it. We bought it on a complete mortgage of $40,000.

Although Goddard was very much a Vermont institution, I was an outsider in Plainfield. I suppose it's because I was rather closely associated with the college. Still, once I became president, there was no other job that I wanted. If you had offered me the presidency of Bennington or Harvard, I wouldn't have even looked at it. To me, Goddard was always an exciting place because there were great possibilities accompanied, of course, by a struggle. The great thing we lacked was money. A depression or a time of economic stringency is not a bad time. There is more likely to be interest in change, conditions being as they are. If I had my druthers I'd take the money, but, if you don't have the money, you have to think hard about what you're doing.

We didn't use the term "innovative." That's an innovative term itself. We were still in the period when progressive education was thought of as being very important. Sarah Lawrence was started about 1927. Bennington was chartered in '25 but didn't open till '32. The Putney School started about 1932. Black Mountain was going when we started.

Currently, there's been this wave of what's been referred to as innovations in the universities. The question is, how many really have thought through the educational principles on which they should be based or the philosophy on which they were developed? So many have simply grafted those arrangements, I'd call them, onto the existing outlook. They retain the credit-examination-bookkeeping system of getting people through college.

LINDA: What's the next innovation, Tim?

My observation is that students tend to be bored, usually around the later elementary years. I would like to reduce the amount of time that kids spend in school and make provision for them to do jobs in the community. Those of us who grew up on farms know that that's where much of the education comes.

I would follow the same policy through college. There'll be some persons who make college a truly intellectual experience, but, for most, that will not be true. It'd be good for them to be in college as long as they find it productive—then drop out, but with a provision for coming back in. This educational process ought to go on throughout life.

IN 1971, STU ROSENFELD, *with his wife, Liz, and their three children, came to Vermont to direct The New School, an alternative elementary school located on Maple Hill in Marshfield. After moving to Hollister Hill, Stu*

*pursued a Ph.D. in education at Harvard while Liz continued to direct The New School.*

## Stu Rosenfeld, 37

I lived in Madison, Wisconsin, for twenty-two years until 1959. Liz and I were already married when I graduated from college. I went into General Electric's Management Training Program. I took a job in G.E.'s Missile and Space Division in Valley Forge, Pennsylvania, for three years. I moved to the Medical Systems Division in Milwaukee in '68.

Going to Milwaukee was like going back home. It was the first time we moved where we knew a lot of people. Most of them were very successful financially—lawyers and dentists and doctors. All had a lot of angles. It was a very competitive, materialistic, close Jewish society. They convinced me to leave G.E. and start my own management-consulting company.

I wasn't liking the business at all. I hated having to sell services I wasn't convinced a small businessman needed. I didn't like the people I was working with. From '70 on I was trying to change our course. I got my master's in education part-time while I was working. I saw education as my way out.

Liz and I took a course in alternative education at the Milwaukee Free University. We started reading Paul Goodman and John Dewey and B. F. Skinner. We met some people at the University of Wisconsin who were starting a free school. We liked the people; we liked the whole concept. We took the kids out of public school.

It was strictly a parent cooperative. Everybody used to come in their jeans and their sweatshirts, and I'd come in with my suit and tie. I was still in my consulting firm. It was a real split in my life. Most of our old friends and family thought we were crazy and needed help. It was very difficult living in Milwaukee and making a change.

For some reason, Vermont was always my ideal of where I wanted to live. About ten or fifteen years ago I saw an old Alfred Hitchcock movie called *The Trouble with Harry*, which took place in Vermont. I was really impressed with the scenery. I drove through the state on a one-day trip to give a talk at G.E.'s plant in Burlington. I knew the state was changing, that dissatisfied city people were moving out here.

We came to Plainfield in August of '71 strictly by chance. Some friends were traveling in New England and heard about this really neat school, called The New School, that was looking for a couple to run it. They called us on the Sunday that we had just driven 2200 miles straight from California. We drove out to Plainfield a week later for the interview.

We were invited to a blintz dinner at a commune that had just broken up, but still had communal dinners. We realized there was some kind of a Jewish community here, which was somewhat important. To go to the barn—it was very rustic—and to sleep on the floor, and to have a communal bathroom everybody walked in and out of while you were in there, freaked us out a little.

It was like nothing we had ever seen before, but we liked the area, the people, the school, and figured that we would probably never find that kind of an opportunity again. We convinced them that we should have the job. It was everything we had expected and wanted. Everything was much less formal here. I got rid of all my suits. I lost thirty pounds almost immediately. Even though the work was hard, it was the first time I didn't dread going into work on a Monday morning.

Coming here, we wanted to be accepted. We tried to fit into people's expectations. I hid the fact I had some money in the stock market until I found out the matriarch of the alternative community had money in the stock market. We were sort of ashamed to have those French-provincial-type tables we had in the city. We wanted to mar them up a little bit. We were happy when our sofa started to wear through.

There's competitiveness around here, but it's not material. It's more of an intellectual one-upmanship: what you read, who you know, what movies you see. You have to know the right things and only in certain areas. The fact that I used to be pretty good in statistics is not valued because people here don't believe in statistics.

Being involved in the school was a perfect way to get involved in the community. But it was also one very small segment of the community—city people who were trying to be country people. Most were from upper-middle-class families. They were well educated. They were giving up a certain kind of material success that maybe people in the country still wanted.

I never had any doubts that I could fit in with the old Vermont people. I was very surprised when I got here. Because of our association with The New School, I was looked at as a dangerous radical. The neighbors across the street wouldn't allow their kids to play with our kids. They felt, as they've told me, that the language was bad, that there was nudity, that the kids had no respect.

At first I felt it was important to bridge this gap. I felt that they were hostile because they didn't understand what we were trying to do. We tried to get to know our neighbors. Up to a point, we did. Since then, I've realized it's only at the surface that they're friendly. They're really very bitter. They don't speak for everybody, but they speak for a large part of the community.

I see the alternative community changing. When we came, people were almost anti-professional. They wanted to live together and relate to each other. They were trying to set up radical, separate organizations and create an alternative. There was a lot of planning for our Utopian future. There's not the same kind of excitement and hope now. People are back to making more marginal changes and working within the system. It's almost a resurgence of getting involved in the establishment. Even the political people are getting more involved in party politics.

I see myself working at the Vermont State Department of Education if I could find a job. I'm much less optimistic about the role of education because I realize schools don't make the changes; they reflect them. Alternative schools might be making kids happier, but they're not the agent of social change. I don't know what is.

I'll be thirty-eight in three weeks. Maybe at some point you have to admit that you're middle-aged. I think it changes your outlook. You start to realize that you haven't got as much time to do the things you wanted to do. You can't be quite as idealistic about the future. You can't have the same kind of dreams.

AS THE OLD REMEMBER THE PAST, *men in their thirties and forties chart the future—economic, political and social. Scott Nielsen, who has a Ph.D. in economics from M.I.T., teaches the physical sciences at Goddard College. The result of Scott's self-education, and that of his students, has been the construction of a windmill behind the house where he lives with his wife, Janet, and their two children.*

## Scott Nielsen, 44

Last fall I attended a social-ecology conference at Goddard. Out of the conference I got excited about alternate sources of energy. The winter term at Goddard I taught a course in energy: the history, the use, the technology of energy; the physics and the scientific principles of energy conversion; how people use energy resources; and how we are likely to get energy in the future. In our lifetime we're going to go through a real energy crisis. We're going to need all kinds of alternatives.

As a challenge I said, "Can I make this house independent of fossil-fuel energy?" Last November I switched over from electric heat to wood heat. In the wintertime we'll heat water with wood. I hope by next spring to be fooling around with a solar hot-water heater to get my water heated in the summertime. This summer I went out to

North Dakota looking for Jacobs' wind electric generators.

Anyone that starts investigating the history of wind generators in this country, learns that Jacobs' was the best generator ever made. He made them from the early '30's until 1956. He was put out of business by rural electrification because it's cheaper to buy power than to generate it yourself. Vermont farmers gave up outhouses as soon as they had the opportunity; they got automobiles; as soon as electricity came along, they took it.

I brought home one windmill tower sixty feet high. The trees around here are fifty feet high. In New England, wind travels about ten miles an hour, which is about the same as in the Midwest. But New England is hilly and woody so that you can't get up into the wind.

I got some batteries from the telephone company. New they would have cost a couple of thousand dollars; I was able to pick them up for scrap value. Each battery weighs about 200 pounds and stands around two feet tall, eight inches wide and fourteen inches high. They're in clear plexiglass cases so that you can see the individual lead plates. They're really beautiful things.

I'm interested in trying to switch over to wind power for two reasons: one, to generate electricity from a non-fossil fuel — the wind will blow forever — but, secondly, a generation from now all of us will have to live with less energy. This wind generator will generate about 300 kilowatt-hours per month. When I had electric heat, I used 3,000 kilowatt-hours per month. Even without electric heat, I've got all kinds of things that are electric: hot water, stove, washer and dryer, dishwasher, lights. It's an all-electric house.

Electricity is one of the most marvelous forms of energy. But I'm not ready to operate at a level extremely removed from technology at this point. I see wind power as an intermediate step going in that direction. In the next thirty years we are going to run up against a number of ecological barriers. If we wait until other systems stop working, it's going to be a horror show.

When people start coming out of the cities without power and without food, they're not going to respect any property laws. They're going to kill. We might be able to survive if enough people try alternatives that are kinder to the earth and use less energy. I see this as an exciting challenge, an experiment. We have to start building Noah's arks for survival.

JIM HIGGINS ("JBLU") LIVES WITH HIS PARTNER, *Jayne Israel, in a small wooden building in a field at the lower end of Hollister Hill. Here he elaborates on the development of his two names and of the food cooperative he organized, the Plainfield Co-op.*

## Jim Higgins ("Jblu"), 27

My double identity came in when I was 100 percent paranoid about the Vietnam War draft. I turned in my draft card and refused induction. My decision was not to go to jail but to go to Canada. I told my draft board I was enrolled in a college in Saskatchewan. It was an appeasement, not only in my own mind, but for everyone connected with me intimately.

I found Canada very cold. I was homesick. I knew I was not where I really wanted to be, and it ate at me. The only thing I could do to ease the pain was to come back and begin a three-year phase of paranoia in this country. I assumed a different set of I.D. cards from a man in California. He fit my features, so I paid him $25 and took his draft card, driver's license and library card.

I was fully content being a traveling carpenter in California. I lived cheaply and did anything that anybody asked just for the experience of learning how to do it. The final resting place was working on a spiral staircase in exchange for room and board. My client—he was a writer, an artist—began to turn me on to left-wing thought-thinking. I had been exposed to it all through college, but it was dormant.

At about the last step of the staircase, I had this very mystical experience which I don't talk about often. I had this realization that I should devote my life, not to indulging myself in this high—which was a very singular relationship between me, my work and my client—but doing something more selfless for people who weren't that fortunate. I moved to Vermont to decide what I was going to do. I loved the countryside, but, more than that, the people who were my old friends were here. From my experience in Canada, that is *the* most important attachment—people.

I felt it was important to change my name so that "Jim Higgins" wasn't known to be in the area—in case somebody came looking. "Jblu" was christened at a ritual at Maple Hill Commune. We were standing in a circle after smoking an appropriate amount of pot and being hazy enough at 5:00 a.m. to give it a spiritual/ritualistic air. We had just thrown the *I Ching* and were humming and chanting and doing all those hippie things you do when you're stoned and feeling very good about the people you're with.

It was quiet in the circle, and I was racking my brains waiting for this inspiration. A dog named Jessie broke into the circle and stood right in the center. I took that as a sign, of course, and connected the name Jessie with the name someone had planted in my head earlier: Blue. So "Jblu" came out of it.

The beautiful part about my phasing into Vermont was that I was a blank. I was 100 percent open. I knew I was going to devote my life to social activism, wherever that would take me, but I didn't know what it would be. It had lots of interesting little false starts.

The first big issue was the hippie invasion of Vermont. The papers were full of these scare headlines: "50,000 Hippies Projected to Invade Vermont This Summer," "Hordes of Hippie Invaders on Their Way." A public organization had called for a state-wide conference of all selectmen to deal with the problem.

What was needed in this *crisis* atmosphere was an idea, a plan. Since no one else was coming up with plans—everyone was just scared—I went out in the woods with my notebook and brainstormed. The result was: Why not connect all these aimless, drifting hippies with farms to share labor for a place to set up camp? And do this with the blessing of the townspeople who would help the connection? I was busy finding farmers who would be interested.

The organization met, and all the heavies in the state were there. After they each gave a little speech about what they were going to do, they asked for people from the floor to comment. I got up and laid out this idea. It was the only idea of the day, so everyone responded to it. We were waiting in June, July. Day after day no hordes of hippies came through the state. Nothing happened! This whole thing was a scare. I realized I'd better start doing something else with my time.

I moved into the recycling field. A recycling drive met my criteria because it demanded that I literally walk the roads, the long country roads here, and sit and talk with people. To perform my function as a change agent, I had to know everybody.

I talked to people about my plan: "We will collect your glass and cans if you will save them. We'll have a depot down in back of the town fire station." The pick-up was the unique feature that had to be incorporated because it played to the lowest denominator of people's energy. You raise the standard, persistently. People were starting to bring stuff by; people were even getting ready to wash their own glass.

Still, I didn't know quite how to think completely. As in every other project I had pursued, there was a flaw. The fatal flaw was no outlets. The stuff built up and built up, and I had eighteen drums of the stuff! And I had twenty drums at Goddard College. I finally made a deal with a local bottler to pick all the stuff up. He said he was going to take it to a recycling depot, but he never did. He dumped it. He said he was going to pay me a dollar a drum, and he never paid me anything. I had paid for all the materials, so I took a big loss. I was *looking* for my next major venture that would draw upon all the mistakes and successes I had had.

During this time I was also working at the Goddard Co-op. I was long into natural foods — four years — and the co-op at Goddard was people-oriented and non-profit. It folded as all co-ops seem to fold when they're based on the volunteer energy of one or two people. I ran into one of the key organizers of the Goddard Co-op, and he said, "Oh, you're going to start the co-op again, aren't cha?" I was known as someone who was interested in those things. At that time I said, "You gotta be kidding, man; that is the biggest hassle in the world. Are you crazy?" He left it at that and we parted.

I sat on the idea for about a month. The more I thought about it, the more I realized that a co-op did all the things I wanted to do: it got people together; it had a natural-foods focus; it self-capitalized; it was a service project; it was open-ended; and it had enough politics. I knew that there was no pivotal service or project in town that got everyone involved. It made sense politically to organize among all the counter-cultural types (you know, my friends) that were up here. And then hope that the co-op would move into the other elements in the community and eventually bring about some kind of — harmony.

I printed up a food list. I had suppliers and a trucking network to plug into. I did a lot of hustling among Goddard faculty, who I knew would be the easiest to get interested, and we had a $400 order. Each month the size increased, demanding greater attention to more and more details, demanding more and more participation. It escalated until it's now $20,000 a month, demanding the full time of six people to run it and the participation of twenty-eight active neighborhood coordinators and the people around *them* who participate. It's succeeding in one of its original functions, which was to mingle people of different backgrounds.

A lot of the neighborhood-coordinators' slots are being filled up by the next line before natives. That was the next line of resistance for the co-op to break down, the resistance of genuine middle America to outside cooperative ideas which still have the label of socialist, communist. These cross-cultural alliances definitely weren't happening before. Times are harder, these alliances are more pressing, and we've grown.

I stumbled my way into my life's work. I'm more than ever interested in the food problem in this area and the country. I'm more than ever interested in the concept of cooperatives for political and economic reasons. Oh, the draft board finally reclassified me, which means I'm currently ineligible to be inducted. Once I started moving among the native Vermonters, "Jblu" had a point of diminishing returns. "Jim Higgins" is phasing back in.

TWO OF RUTH BUXTON LUMBRA'S BROTHERS, *Roy and Claiton Buxton, joined us for a second interview to reminisce about their boyhood on the hill. Roy worked for Green Mountain Power Corporation, eventually becoming a district manager. Claiton, called "Babe," served the State of Vermont for forty-eight years, including twelve years as the Sergeant-at-Arms in the Vermont Legislature. Both men are now retired.*

## Roy and Claiton Buxton, 69 and 66

ROY: In the fall of the year, right after haying, we would sleep in the barn on the new-mown hay. We'd spread out horse blankets and put our bedding on top. 'Twas soft and 'twas nice in the nice soft hay.

CLAITON: Depending on how you look at it. In the morning you'd be down in a hole, your back broken, wringin' wet with sweat from the heat in the hay.

Today people cut corn into silos for feed, but our corn was cut just before the frost. Eventually, it would be loaded on wagons and stacked in barns. Along about early November, as I remember it, it would be laid on the floor. You'd husk it right on the stalk. The empty stalk would be thrown out for bedding, while the corn would go into a crib to dry further and keep all winter.

It was a tedious job, but having the neighbors in helped. The old folks would be telling yarns, like we're doing today, and the kids would listen and maybe snicker at a little prank. Later in the evening, the lady of the house would have some pumpkin pies and maybe some sweet cider and cookies.

My father's generation made even more of a social out of it. The young men and women would husk for a while, and if one found a red ear—

ROY: (They were smuggled in.)

CLAITON: —he could kiss a girl. Quite often back then they'd wind up the husking with a square dance when they cleaned out a place on the floor.

ROY: Speaking as a country boy, Saturday night was a big time to go to town. The Plainfield Hotel had quite a hall where we used to play basketball during the winter. In the summer there was a swimming hole or baseball.

CLAITON: Back then, 'most every town had its local baseball team. There was a lot of rivalry between towns. My brother spoke of the swimming hole. The swimming hole was a deep spot in the river. The girls wouldn't go in, because, as a matter of fact, it was skinny-dipping. No one dreamt that the water wasn't fit to swim in.

ROY: When we'd exhausted ourselves, it was time to go home. We used to think ten o'clock would be quite late. We walked about two and a half miles from town.

You were leaving a good time behind you, and as you got nearer and nearer home, there was a sense of getting home. You would pass the last neighbor; the dogs would come out and bark. You'd come to the mailbox—'twould be the first thing that was yours—then you'd come to a line of fence, then you would come to the pasture, then you'd come to the orchard. There was a big stone that we used to play on, then you'd turn into your yard. You were coming to the heart of home. You were coming to what was yours.

IT SEEMED FITTING *for Miff Keene to have the last word.*

## Miff Keene, 53

Yes, it's come again as it always has. My leaves are turnin' colors and the apples are turnin' ripe. Soon the geese will go south, and the cattle will have to be in the barn. Some of the summer work will be over, and some of it will never be done.

When we go up the road, we may meet a neighbor we haven't seen for a long time and have a chance to speak. Perhaps at deer-season time we can have a few hours to hunt; maybe we can't. That's the way it is every year.

But then the snow comes. You set beside your window, if you have the chance, and watch it fall down like goose feathers all over the place. Your cars are covered with snow. You clean them off and shovel them out. They won't start. Anyway, it's been another year.